Create paradise with 24 quilts in exotic fabrics!

Best of Fons&Porter
Batik QUILTS

LEISURE ARTS

the art of everyday living

www.leisurearts.com

FONS & PORTER STAFF
Editors-in-Chief Marianne Fons and Liz Porter

Editor Jean Nolte
Associate Editor Diane Tomlinson
Technical Editor Marjon Schaefer
Technical Writer Kristine Peterson

Art Director Tony Jacobson

Interactive Editor Mandy Couture
Sewing Specialist Cindy Hathaway

Contributing Photographers Dean Tanner, Katie Downey, Craig Anderson
Contributing Photo Assistant DeElda Wittmack

Publisher Kristi Loeffelholz
Advertising Manager Cristy Adamski
Retail Manager Sharon Hart
Web Site Manager Phillip Zacharias
Customer Service Manager Tiffiny Bond
Fons & Porter Staff Megan Johansen, Cynde Keating, Laura Saner, Yvonne Smith, Anne Welker, Karla Wesselmann

New Track Media LLC
President and CEO Stephen J. Kent
Chief Financial Officer Mark F. Arnett
President, Book Publishing W. Budge Wallis
Vice President/Publishing Director Joel P. Toner
Vice President/Group Publisher Tina Battock
Vice President, Circulation Nicole McGuire
Vice President, Production Barbara Schmitz
Production Manager Dominic M. Taormina
Production Coordinator Amanda Booher
IT Manager Denise Donnarumma
Renewal and Billing Manager Nekeya Dancy
Online Subscriptions Manager Jodi Lee

Our Mission Statement
Our goal is for you to enjoy making quilts as much as we do.

LEISURE ARTS STAFF
Vice President of Editorial Susan White Sullivan
Creative Art Director Katherine Laughlin
Special Projects Director Susan Frantz Wiles
Prepress Technician Stephanie Johnson

President and Chief Executive Officer Rick Barton
Senior Vice President of Operations Jim Dittrich
Vice President of Finance Fred F. Pruss
Vice President of Sales-Retail Books Martha Adams
Vice President of Mass Market Bob Bewighouse
Vice President of Technology and Planning Laticia Mull Dittrich
Controller Francis Caple
Information Technology Director Brian Roden
Director of E-Commerce Mark Hawkins
Manager of E-Commerce Robert Young
Retail Customer Service Manager Stan Raynor

Library of Congress Control Number: 2013938884
ISBN-13/EAN: 978-1-4647-0869-5

We're thrilled to bring you this collection of some of our favorite batik quilts! The projects included are among our most popular of all time. In this book, you'll find patterns for all skill levels. Enjoy the beautiful photography as you browse through the pages to find the project that's just right for you. Whether you want to make a small quilt, a bed-size one, or something in between, you're sure to find plenty to love. Our trademarked *Sew Easy* lessons will guide you via step-by-step photography through any project-specific special techniques. We think you'll have fun making these batik beauties for your home or to give as gifts to family and friends.

Happy quilting,

Marianne + Liz

Table of Contents

28

Under the Sea	6
Split Rail Fence	12
Imperial Diamonds	16
Circles, Circles	22
Batik Magic	28
Prairie Skies	32
Blue Bayou	36
Crossed Kayaks	42
September Leaves	48
Woven Wonder	56
On the Dark Side	60
Tucson Sunset	64
Triangle Surprise	68
Tranquility	72
Horse Play	76
Charming Diamonds	82
Sailing	88
Sunflowers	92
Night Blooms	98
Gold Rush	104
Baby Blue Mini	108

82

32

Candy Flowers   110

Graceful Ladies   114

Double Wedding Ring   120

Behind the Batiks   128

Techniques

Sew Easy: Cutting Curved Pieces   27

Sew Easy: Piecing Curves   27

Sew Easy: Clamshell Units   54

Sew Easy: Working with 60-Degree

    Diamonds   86

Sew Easy: Using Paintstiks® on Fabric   96

Sew Easy: Bobbin Work   118

Sew Easy: Piecing Double Wedding

    Ring   124

Sew Easy: Binding Uneven Edges   126

Behind the Batiks   **128**

General Instructions   **132**

68

56

108

Under the Sea

Sandi Irish used a beautiful collection of batiks to make this striking quilt. The greens and teals, shaded from light in the center to darker at the corners, add to the watery effect. Although she used only one easy block, by carefully placing the colors, she created a Snail's Trail design.

PROJECT RATING: INTERMEDIATE

Size: 86" × 103"

Blocks: 80 (6") blocks

MATERIALS

⅝ yard green batik #1

1 yard green batik #2

1⅛ yards green batik #3

1 yard green batik #4

½ yard green batik #5

½ yard green batik #6

¾ yard green batik #7

5 yards teal batik #1 for blocks, outer border, and binding

1½ yards teal batik #2

1½ yards teal batik #3

½ yard teal batik #4 for inner border

7⅞ yards backing fabric

Queen-size quilt batting

Cutting

Measurements include ¼" seam allowances. Border strips are exact length needed. You may want to make them longer to allow for piecing variations.

From green batik #1, cut:

- 1 (9¾"-wide) strip. From strip, cut 2 (9¾") squares. Cut squares in half diagonally in both directions to make 8 quarter-square setting triangles.
- 1 (3⅞"-wide) strip. From strip, cut 8 (3⅞") squares. Cut squares in half diagonally to make 16 half-square C triangles.
- 2 (2⅝"-wide) strips. From strips, cut 16 (2⅝") B squares.

From green batik #2, cut:

- 1 (9¾"-wide) strip. From strip, cut 2 (9¾") squares. Cut squares in half diagonally in both directions to make 8 quarter-square setting triangles.
- 1 (6½"-wide) strip. From strip, cut 4 (6½") A squares.
- 2 (3⅞"-wide) strips. From strips, cut 16 (3⅞") squares. Cut squares in half diagonally to make 32 half-square C triangles.
- 3 (2⅝"-wide) strips. From strips, cut 32 (2⅝") B squares.

From green batik #3, cut:

- 2 (6½"-wide) strips. From strips, cut 12 (6½") A squares.
- 3 (3⅞"-wide) strips. From strips, cut 24 (3⅞") squares. Cut squares in half diagonally to make 48 half-square C triangles.
- 4 (2⅝"-wide) strips. From strips, cut 48 (2⅝") B squares.

From green batik #4, cut:

- 2 (6½"-wide) strips. From strips, cut 8 (6½") A squares.
- 2 (3⅞"-wide) strips. From strips, cut 16 (3⅞") squares. Cut squares in half diagonally to make 32 half-square C triangles.
- 3 (2⅝"-wide) strips. From strips, cut 32 (2⅝") B squares.

From green batik #5, cut:

- 1 (6½"-wide) strip. From strip, cut 4 (6½") A squares.
- 1 (3⅞"-wide) strip. From strip, cut 8 (3⅞") squares. Cut squares in half diagonally to make 16 half-square C triangles.
- 2 (2⅝"-wide) strips. From strips, cut 16 (2⅝") B squares.

From green batik #6, cut:

- 1 (6½"-wide) strip. From strip, cut 1 (6½") A square.
- 1 (3⅞"-wide) strip. From strip, cut 2 (3⅞") squares. Cut squares in half diagonally to make 4 half-square C triangles.
- 1 (2⅝"-wide) strip. From strip, cut 4 (2⅝") B squares.

From green batik #7, cut:

- 1 (6½"-wide) strip. From strip, cut 4 (6½") A squares.
- 1 (5⅛"-wide) strip. From strip, cut 2 (5⅛") squares. Cut squares in half diagonally to make 4 half-square corner setting triangles.
- 1 (3⅞"-wide) strip. From strip, cut 8 (3⅞") squares. Cut squares in half diagonally to make 16 half-square C triangles.
- 2 (2⅝"-wide) strips. From strips, cut 16 (2⅝") B squares.

From teal batik #1, cut:

- 1 (9¾"-wide) strip. From strip, cut 1 (9¾") square. Cut square in half diagonally in both directions to make 4 quarter-square setting triangles (2 are extra).
- 10 (8½"-wide) strips. Piece strips to make 2 (8½" × 87½") side outer borders and 2 (8½" × 86½") top and bottom outer borders.
- 3 (6½"-wide) strips. From strips, cut 14 (6½") A squares.
- 3 (3⅞"-wide) strips. From strips, cut 30 (3⅞") squares. Cut squares in half diagonally to make 60 half-square C triangles.
- 4 (2⅝"-wide) strips. From strips, cut 60 (2⅝") B squares.
- 11 (2¼"-wide) strips for binding.

From teal batik #2, cut:

- 1 (9¾"-wide) strip From strip, cut 2 (9¾") squares. Cut squares in half diagonally in both directions to make 8 quarter-square setting triangles (2 are extra).
- 2 (6½"-wide) strips. From strips, cut 12 (6½") A squares.
- 3 (3⅞"-wide) strips. From strips, cut 30 (3⅞") squares. Cut squares in half diagonally to make 60 half-square C triangles.
- 4 (2⅝"-wide) strips. From strips, cut 60 (2⅝") B squares.

From teal batik #3, cut:

- 1 (9¾"-wide) strip. From strip, cut 2 (9¾") squares. Cut squares in half diagonally in both directions to make 8 quarter-square setting triangles.
- 2 (6½"-wide) strips. From strips, cut 8 (6½") A squares.
- 3 (3⅞"-wide) strips. From strips, cut 24 (3⅞") squares. Cut squares in half diagonally to make 48 half-square C triangles.
- 4 (2⅝"-wide) strips. From strips, cut 48 (2⅝") B squares.

From teal batik #4, cut:

- 9 (1½"-wide) strips. Piece strips to make 2 (1½" × 85½") side inner borders and 2 (1½" × 70½") top and bottom inner borders.

Block Assembly

1. Lay out 1 green batik #7 B square, 2 green batik #1 B squares, and 1 green batik #2 B square as shown in *Four Patch Unit Assembly Diagrams*. Join squares to make 1 Four Patch Unit.

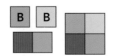

Four Patch Unit Assembly Diagrams

2. Lay out Four Patch Unit, 1 green batik #7 C triangle, 2 green batik #1 C triangles, and 1 green batik #2 C triangle as shown in *Block 1 Assembly Diagram*. Join triangles to Four Patch Unit to complete Block 1 (*Block 1 Diagram*).

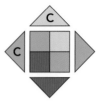 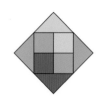

Block 1 Assembly Diagram   Block 1 Diagram

3. Referring to *Block Diagrams*, repeat steps #1 and #2 to make make Blocks 1–8 in quantities indicated.

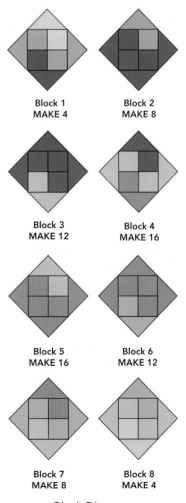

Block 1
MAKE 4

Block 2
MAKE 8

Block 3
MAKE 12

Block 4
MAKE 16

Block 5
MAKE 16

Block 6
MAKE 12

Block 7
MAKE 8

Block 8
MAKE 4

Block Diagrams

Quilt Top Assembly Diagram

Quilt Assembly

1. Lay out A squares, blocks, and setting triangles as shown in *Quilt Top Assembly Diagram.*

2. Join into diagonal rows; join rows to complete quilt center.

3. Add teal batik #4 side inner borders to quilt center. Add top and bottom inner borders to quilt.

4. Repeat for teal batik #1 outer borders.

5. Join 1 green batik #7 A square, 3 green batik #7 C triangles, and 3 green batik #7 B squares as shown in *Corner Assembly Diagrams*. Make 4 Corner Units.

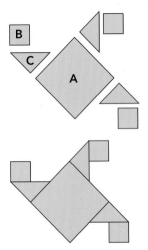

Corner Assembly Diagrams

6. Press outer seam allowances of Corner Units toward wrong side. Lay 1 Corner Unit atop quilt top, matching seam line of Corner Unit with seam line of corner setting triangle.

7. Appliqué Corner Unit to quilt top as shown in photo on page 11. Repeat for remaining corner units.

Finishing

1. Divide backing into 3 (2⅝-yard) lengths. Join panels lengthwise. Seams will run horizontally.

2. Layer backing, batting, and quilt top; baste. Quilt as desired. Quilt shown was quilted with reel designs in the quilt center and an allover wave design in the outer border *(Quilting Diagram)*.

3. Join 2¼"-wide teal batik #1 strips into 1 continuous piece for straight-grain French-fold binding. Add binding to quilt.

Quilting Diagram

DESIGNER

Sandi Irish has been quilting for over twenty years, designing quilts for fabric companies and making commissioned works. She creates her own designs and adapts traditional patterns to her style for her company, Irish Chain. ✳

Split Rail Fence

Tony Jacobson designed this totally modern quilt using his endless stash of batiks. Use your favorite batiks and the versatile Fons & Porter Large Wedge Template to make your own version of this traditionally inspired Split Rail Fence pattern.

PROJECT RATING: EASY

Size: 67½" × 90"

Blocks: 108 (7½") blocks

MATERIALS

31 fat quarters★ assorted batiks

Fons & Porter Large Wedge Template or template material

5½ yards backing fabric

Twin-size quilt batting

★fat quarter = 18" × 20"

Cutting

If you are not using the Large Wedge Template, make a template from the pattern on page 14. Measurements include ¼" seam allowances.

From each fat quarter, cut:

• 2 (8" × 20") strips. From strips, cut 14 Wedges.

NOTE: Place the **NARROW** end of Large Wedge Template even with edge of strip when cutting wedges.

From remainder of each of 20 fat quarters, cut:

• 1 (2¼"-wide) strip for binding.

Block Assembly

1. Choose 2 pairs of matching wedges.

2. Join wedges as shown in *Block Assembly Diagrams.* Trim sides of unit as shown to complete 1 block *(Block Diagram)*.

3. Make 108 blocks.

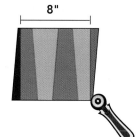

8"

Block Assembly Diagrams

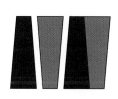

Block Diagram

Quilt Assembly

1. Lay out blocks as shown in *Quilt Top Assembly Diagram* on page 14.

2. Join blocks into rows; join rows to complete quilt center.

Finishing

1. Divide backing into 2 (2¾-yard) lengths. Cut 1 piece in half lengthwise to make 2 narrow panels. Join 1 narrow panel to each side of wider panel; press seam allowances toward narrow panels.

2. Layer backing, batting, and quilt top; baste. Quilt as desired. Quilt shown was quilted with continuous curve flower designs and meandering *(Quilting Diagram on page 15)*.

3. Join 2¼"-wide assorted strips into 1 continuous piece for straight-grain French-fold binding. Add binding to quilt.

Quilt Top Assembly Diagram

SIZE OPTIONS

	Queen (90" × 105")	King (112½" × 112½")
Blocks	168	225
Setting	12 × 14	15 × 15

MATERIALS

Assorted batiks	48 fat quarters	65 fat quarters
Backing Fabric	8¼ yards	10⅛ yards
Batting	Queen-Size	King-Size

Wedge Template

 WEB EXTRA

Go to www.FonsandPorter.com/splitrailfencesizes to download *Quilt Top Assembly Diagrams* and cutting directions for these size options.

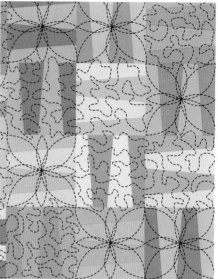

Quilting Diagram

DESIGNER

Tony Jacobson is the Art Director for *Easy Quilts*. He and his wife, Jeanne, enjoy many of the same passions—decorating, gardening, theater, and, of course, quilting. They share their home in Winterset with two dogs, Harley and Howie, and one cat, Barnaby. ✳

TRIED & TRUE

This block is so versatile. Just remember that each block needs a light and a dark fabric for contrast. We stitched our blocks using fabrics from the Cattails and Clover collection by Kansas Troubles Quilters for Moda.

Imperial Diamonds

Love of Quilting editor Jean Nolte designed this strippy quilt to use a collection of pre-cut batiks. She made it easier by strip piecing the small square sections and borders.

PROJECT RATING: INTERMEDIATE

Size: 97" × 108"

MATERIALS

1 package of assorted dark batik 10" squares [or 28 (10") squares]

1 package of assorted 2½"-wide dark batik strips [or 17 (2½"-wide) strips]

4¾ yards cream batik for background

2⅞ yards purple batik for sashing and narrow borders

3¾ yards multicolor batik for borders and binding

Fons & Porter Half & Quarter Ruler (optional)

9 yards backing fabric

King-size quilt batting

Cutting

Measurements include ¼" seam allowances. Instruction are written for using the Fons & Porter Half & Quarter Ruler. If not using this ruler, follow cutting **NOTE**.

From assorted dark batik 10" squares, cut a total of:

• 112 (4½") A squares.

From cream batik, cut:

• 7 (4½"-wide) strips. From strips, cut 52 (4½") A squares.

• 13 (3½"-wide) strips. From strips, cut 112 quarter-square B triangles. Save beginning corner triangles from 8 strips to make 16 C triangles.

  NOTE: If not using the Fons & Porter Half & Quarter Ruler, cut 6 (7¼"-wide) strips and 1 (4"-wide) strip. From 7¼"-wide strips, cut 28 (7¼") squares. Cut squares in half diagonally in both directions to make 112 quarter-square B triangles. From 4"-wide strip, cut 8 (4") squares. Cut squares in half diagonally to make 16 half-square C triangles (B and C triangles are slightly oversized).

• 36 (2½"-wide) strips. From 2 strips, cut 18 (2½") D squares. Remaining strips are for strip sets.

From purple batik, cut:

• 20 (1½"-wide) **lengthwise** strips. From strips, cut 2 (1½" × 96⅝") side border #4, 2 (1½" × 89") side border #2, 2 (1½" × 87⅜") top and bottom border #4, 10 (1½" × 79¾") vertical sashing strips, 2 (1½" × 79¾") top and bottom border #2, and 2 (1½" × 69⅞") horizontal sashing strips.

From multicolor batik, cut:

• 11 (2¼"-wide) strips for binding.

• 4 (5½"-wide) **lengthwise** strips. From strips, cut 2 (5½" × 98⅝") side border #5 and 2 (5½" × 97⅜") top and bottom border #5.

• 2 (4⅜"-wide) **lengthwise** strips. From strips, cut 2 (4⅜" × 81¾") side border #1.

• 2 (4⅛"-wide) **lengthwise** strips. From strips, cut 2 (4⅛" × 77¾") top and bottom border #1.

Panel Assembly

1. Join 2 dark batik A squares, 1 cream batik A square, and 2 cream batik B triangles as shown in *Panel Unit Diagram*. Trim points of B triangles even with A squares. Make 44 panel units.

Panel Unit Diagram

2. Lay out 3 dark batik A squares, 1 cream batik A square, 3 cream batik B triangles, and 2 cream batik C triangles as shown in *Corner Unit Assembly Diagram*. Join into diagonal rows; join rows to make 1 corner unit *(Corner Unit Diagram)*. Make 8 corner units.

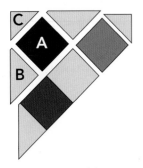

Corner Unit Assembly Diagram

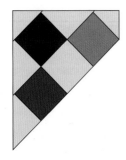

Corner Unit Diagram

3. Referring to *Quilt Top Assembly Diagram*, on page 19, lay out 11 panel units and 2 corner units. Join to complete 1 panel. Trim ¼" outside points of dark batik squares on all sides. Make 4 panels.

Pieced Sashing and Border Assembly

1. Join 1 dark batik strip and 2 cream batik strips as shown in *Strip Set Diagram*. Make 17 strip sets. From strip sets, cut 264 (2½"-wide) segments.

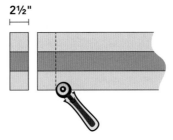

Strip Set Diagram

2. Referring to *Quilt Top Assembly Diagram*, lay out 28 segments and 2 cream batik D squares. Join to make 1 pieced sashing unit.

3. Stitch ⅛" away from points of dark batik squares on all sides as shown in *Stay Stitching Diagram*.

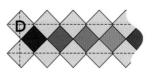

Stay Stitching Diagram

Sew Smart™

Staystitching stabilizes bias edges of triangles to keep the pieced unit from stretching. —Jean

4. Trim sashing unit ¼" outside points of dark batik squares as shown in *Trimming Diagram*. Make 5 pieced sashing units.

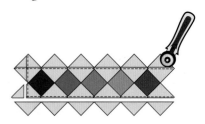

Trimming Diagram

5. In the same manner, make 2 pieced side border #3 using 32 segments and 2 cream batik D squares in each, and 2 top and bottom border #3 using 30 segments and 2 cream batik D squares in each.

6. Referring to *Quilt Top Assembly Diagram*, join 1 purple vertical sashing strip to each side of 1 sashing unit to complete 1 pieced sashing. Make 5 pieced sashings.

Quilt Assembly

1. Lay out panels, pieced sashings, and purple horizontal sashing strips as shown in *Quilt Top Assembly Diagram*.

2. Join panels and pieced sashings. Add purple horizontal sashing strips to top and bottom to complete quilt center.

3. Add 1 multicolor side border #1 to each side of quilt center. Add top and bottom border #1 to quilt.

4. Repeat for borders #2 through #5.

#5

#4

#3

#2

#1

Quilt Top Assembly Diagram

Finishing

1. Divide backing into 3 (3-yard) lengths. Join panels lengthwise. Seams will run horizontally.

2. Layer backing, batting, and quilt top; baste. Quilt as desired. Quilt shown was quilted in the ditch and with diagonal lines in the panels and multicolor print borders *(Quilting Diagram)*.

3. Join 2¼"-wide multicolor strips into 1 continuous piece for straight-grain French-fold binding. Add binding to quilt. ✳

Quilting Diagram

DESIGNER

Jean Nolte is the Editor of all the Fons & Porter magazines, and is also the Editorial Director of "Love of Quilting" on public television. She has been quilting for over thirty years, and is always excited to try a new technique. Her fabric stash contains more yardage than she could possibly use in a lifetime, but she is having lots of fun trying. When not quilting, she loves to travel, knit, or spend time with her family.

QUILT BY **Karen Weber.**

Circles, Circles

Karen Weber used an assortment of fat quarters to make her batik quilt. Use Fons & Porter Curved Seam Templates to make cutting curved pieces easier. See our *Sew Easy* lesson on page 27 for instructions.

PROJECT RATING: EASY

Size: 52" × 58½"

Blocks: 72 (6½") blocks

MATERIALS

36 fat quarters★ assorted batiks

3¼ yards backing fabric

Fons & Porter Curved Seam Templates (optional)

Twin-size quilt batting

★fat quarter = 18" × 20"

Cutting

Measurements include ¼" seam allowances. If not using the Fons & Porter Curved Seam Templates, make templates from patterns on page 25.

From each fat quarter, cut:

• 2 (7"-wide) strips. From strips, cut 4 (7") squares.

From remainders of fat quarters, cut a total of:

• 14 (2¼"-wide) strips for binding.

Block Assembly

1. Referring to *Sew Easy: Cutting Curved Pieces* on page 27, cut pieces for 1 block.

2. Referring to *Sew Easy: Piecing Curves* on page 27, join pieces to complete a block *(Block Diagrams)*. Make 72 blocks.

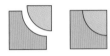

Block Diagrams

Quilt Assembly

1. Lay out blocks as shown in *Quilt Top Assembly Diagram.*

2. Join blocks into rows; join rows to complete quilt top.

Finishing

1. Divide backing into 2 (1⅝-yard) lengths. Join panels lengthwise. Seam will run horizontally.

2. Layer backing, batting, and quilt top; baste. Quilt as desired. Quilt shown was quilted with assorted circles *(Quilting Diagram)*.

3. Join 2¼"-wide batik strips into 1 continuous piece for straight-grain French-fold binding. Add binding to quilt.

Quilt Top Assembly Diagram

Quilting Diagram

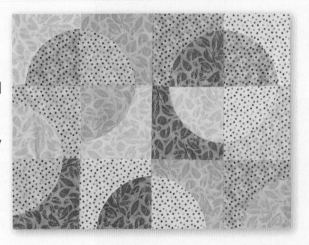

TRIED & TRUE

This pattern adapts nicely to the polka dots and watercolor prints from The Cat Party collection by Red Rooster.

SIZE OPTIONS

	Twin (65" × 91")	Full (84½" × 91")	Queen (91" × 104")
Blocks	140	182	224
Setting	10 × 14	13 × 14	14 × 16

MATERIALS

Assorted Batiks	70 fat quarters	91 fat quarters	112 fat quarters
Backing Fabric	5½ yards	7½ yards	8¼ yards
Batting	Full-size	Queen-size	King-size

WEB EXTRA

Go to www.FonsandPorter.com/circlessizes to download *Quilt Top Assembly Diagrams* for these size options.

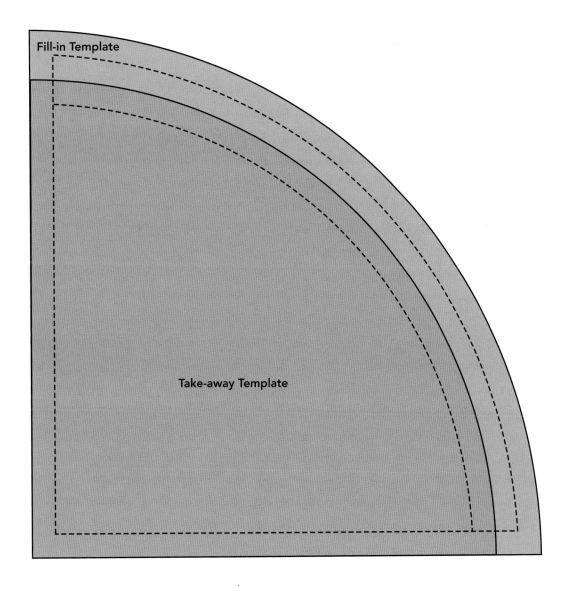

Fill-in Template

Take-away Template

DESIGNER

Karen Weber began quilting in 1999, and hasn't stopped. She loves to make quilts for her family and friends, and enjoys everything from designing quilts to quilting them on her mid-arm machine. ✳

Cutting Curved Pieces

Easily cut the pieces for *Circles, Circles* on page 22 using the Fons & Porter Curved Seam Templates.

1. Cut 1 (7") square from each of 2 contrasting fabrics.
2. Position large red take-away template in 1 corner of square you want to be the background piece. Cut along curved edge of template *(Photo A)*. Either discard the quarter-circle shape or save it to use as a scrap.
3. Position the large gray fill-in template on the other square and cut along the curved edge *(Photo B)* to make a quarter-circle piece. Either discard the remaining portion of the square or save it to use as a scrap.

Piecing Curves

Follow these instructions to piece perfect curves.

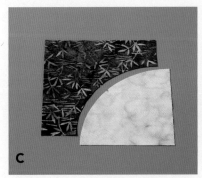

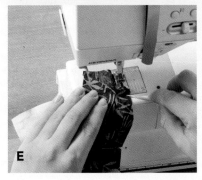

1. Mark center of curve on both background and quarter-circle pieces by folding in half and creasing or by making a small clip *(Photo C)*.
2. Working with background piece on top, pin at curve centers, taking a small bite with the pin. Pin at end of seam, taking a deep bite with the pin *(Photo D)*.
3. Align pieces at beginning of seam. Stitch to middle of curve. Use your fingertips, a stiletto, or a wooden skewer to help keep curved edges aligned as you sew *(Photo E)*.
4. Leaving needle in fabric, raise presser foot. Adjust top fabric away from you toward the area you have already sewn *(Photo F)*.
5. Align curved edges for second half of seam and stitch to about 1" from end of seam. Stop again and adjust top fabric to align ending edges.
6. Gently press seam allowances toward background piece.

Batik Magic

You'll enjoy making this eye-catching quilt. Designer Nancy Mahoney used batiks in a vivid purple and green color combination, but any pairing would make a striking quilt.

PROJECT RATING: EASY
Size: 60" × 72"
Blocks: 20 (12") blocks

MATERIALS

⅜ yard each of 9 assorted dark
  purple batiks
⅜ yard each of 9 assorted medium
  green batiks
1⅜ yards black batik for borders
  and binding
3¾ yards backing fabric
Twin-size quilt batting

Cutting

Measurements include ¼" seam allowances. Border strips are exact length needed. You may want to make them longer to allow for piecing variations.

From assorted dark purple batiks, cut a total of:

- 22 (2½"-wide) strips. From strips, cut 40 (2½" × 6½") A rectangles, 100 (2½" × 4½") B rectangles, and 40 (2½") C squares.

- 11 (1½"-wide) strips. From 1 strip, cut 8 (1½" × 3½") D rectangles. Remaining strips are for strip sets.

From assorted medium green batiks, cut a total of:

- 22 (2½"-wide) strips. From strips, cut 40 (2½" × 6½") A rectangles, 100 (2½" × 4½") B rectangles, and 40 (2½") C squares.

- 11 (1½"-wide) strips. From 1 strip, cut 8 (1½" × 3½") D rectangles. Remaining strips are for strip sets.

From black batik, cut:

- 7 (2½"-wide) strips. Piece strips to make 2 (2½" × 68½") side outer borders and 2 (2½" × 60½") top and bottom outer borders.

- 8 (2¼"-wide) strips for binding.

- 6 (1½"-wide) strips. Piece strips to make 2 (1½" × 60½") side inner borders and 2 (1½" × 50½") top and bottom inner borders.

Block Assembly

1. Lay out 2 green A rectangles, 3 green B rectangles, 2 purple B rectangles, and 2 purple C squares as shown in *Block Unit Diagrams*. Join into sections; join sections to complete 1 green Block Unit. Make 20 green Block Units.

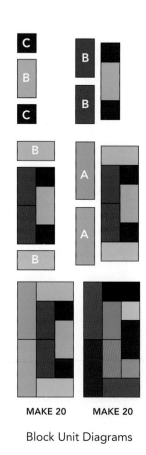

MAKE 20   **MAKE 20**

Block Unit Diagrams

2. In the same manner, make 20 purple Block Units using 2 purple A rectangles, 3 purple B rectangles, 2 green B rectangles, and 2 green C squares in each.

3. Lay out 1 green Block Unit and 1 purple Block Unit as shown in *Block Assembly Diagram*. Join to complete 1 block *(Block Diagram)*. Make 20 blocks.

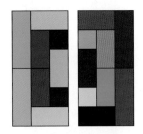

Block Assembly Diagram

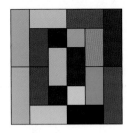

Block Diagram

Pieced Border Assembly

1. Join 5 green strips and 5 purple strips as shown in *Strip Set Diagram*. Make 2 strip sets. From strip sets, cut 22 (3½"-wide) segments.

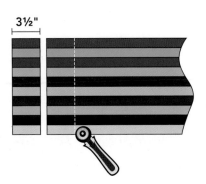

Strip Set Diagram

Sew **Smart**™

When joining strips for strip sets, alternate sewing direction from strip to strip. This keeps strip sets straight. —Marianne

2. Referring to *Quilt Top Assembly Diagram*, join 6 segments, 1 purple D rectangle, and 1 green D rectangle to make 1 pieced side border. Make 2 pieced side borders.

3. In the same manner, join 5 segments, 3 purple D rectangles, and 3 green D rectangles to make pieced top border. Repeat for pieced bottom border.

Quilt Assembly

1. Lay out blocks as shown in *Quilt Top Assembly Diagram*. Join into rows; join rows to complete quilt center.

2. Add black side inner borders to quilt center. Add black top and bottom inner borders to quilt.

3. Repeat for pieced middle borders and black outer borders.

Finishing

1. Divide backing into 2 (1⅞-yard) lengths. Join panels lengthwise. Seam will run horizontally.

2. Layer backing, batting, and quilt top; baste. Quilt as desired. Quilt shown was quilted with an allover shell design in blocks and dart designs in borders *(Quilting Diagram on page 31)*.

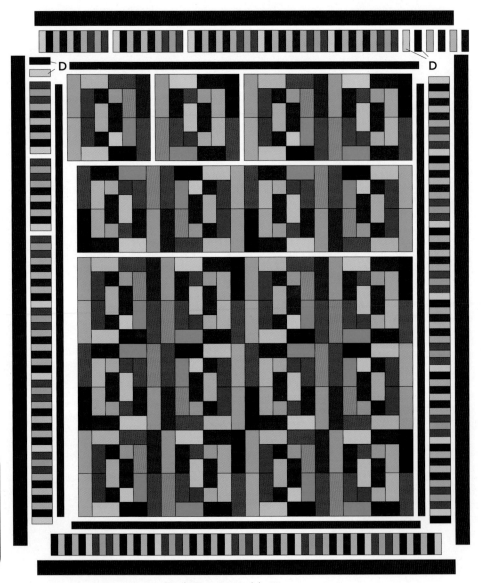

Quilt Top Assembly Diagram

Quilting Diagram

3. Join 2¼"-wide black strips into 1 continuous piece for straight-grain French-fold binding. Add binding to quilt.

TRIED & TRUE

This block is ideal for using precut 2½"-wide strips. We used a Jelly Roll from The Wild Rose collection by Blackbird Designs for Moda.

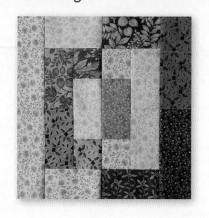

DESIGNER

Author, teacher, fabric designer, and award-winning quiltmaker Nancy Mahoney has enjoyed making quilts for more than twenty years. She enjoys combining traditional blocks and updated techniques to create dazzling quilts. Nancy has authored twelve books, all published by Martingale & Company.

Prairie Skies

Quiltmaker Sandra Holmes used batik fabrics for her version of a quilt called *Prairie Queen*, made by Gerry Sweem. Triangle-squares and strip sets make easy work of the seaming portions in the blocks.

PROJECT RATING: INTERMEDIATE

Size: 84½" × 84½"

Blocks: 40 (9") Prairie Skies blocks

MATERIALS

20 fat quarters* medium/dark batiks for blocks, sashing, and border

4 fat eighths** medium/dark batiks for sashing and border

3 fat eighths** light batiks for sashing squares

5 yards beige batik for background

¾ yard medium batik for binding

7½ yards backing fabric

Queen-size quilt batting

*fat quarter = 18" × 20"

**fat eighth = 9" × 20"

Cutting

Measurements include ¼" seam allowances.

From each medium/dark batik fat quarter, cut:

- 1 (3⅞"-wide) strip. From strip, cut 4 (3⅞") A squares and 1 (3½") B square.

- 1 (3½"-wide) strip. From strip, cut 1 (3½") B square. From remainder of strip, cut 2 (1⁹⁄₁₆"-wide) strips for strip sets. (1⁹⁄₁₆" is halfway between 1½" and 1⅝" on your ruler.)

- 3 (2½"-wide) strips. From strips, cut 6 (2½" × 9½") D rectangles for sashing strips and border.

From each medium/dark batik fat eighth, cut:

- 3 (2½"-wide) strips. From strips, cut 1 (2½" × 15") F corner sashing strip and 3 (2½" × 9½") D rectangles for sashing strips and border.

From each light batik fat eighth, cut:

- 3 (2½"-wide) strips. From strips, cut 21 (2½") E squares.

From beige batik, cut:

- 3 (16¾") strips. From strips, cut 5 (16¾") squares. Cut squares in half diagonally in both directions to make 20 quarter-square setting triangles.

- 8 (3⅞"-wide) strips. From strips, cut 80 (3⅞") A squares.

- 20 (1⁹⁄₁₆") strips. Cut strips in half to make 40 (1⁹⁄₁₆" × 20") strips for strip sets.

- 20 (2⅜"-wide) strips. From strips, cut 320 (2⅜") squares. Cut squares in half diagonally to make 640 half-square C triangles.

From medium batik, cut:

- 9 (2¼"-wide) strips for binding.

Block Assembly

1. Choose 1 matching set of 2 medium/dark A squares. Place 1 background A square atop 1 medium/dark A square, right sides facing. Referring to *Triangle-Square Diagrams* draw a diagonal line from corner to corner on wrong side of light square. Stitch ¼" from drawn line on each side.

Triangle-Square Diagrams

2. Cut on drawn line to make 2 triangle-squares. Press seam allowances toward dark fabric. Make 4 triangle-squares.

3. Referring to *Strip Set Diagram*, join 1 background and 1 medium/dark 1⁹⁄₁₆"-wide strip to form a strip set. Press seam toward dark fabric. From strip set, cut 8 (1⁹⁄₁₆"-wide) segments.

1⁹⁄₁₆"

Strip Set Diagram

4. Join 2 segments to make a four patch. Make 4 four patches.

Four Patch Diagrams

5. Referring to *Four Patch Unit Diagrams*, join 1 C triangle to each side of four patch. Press seam allowances toward triangles. Make 4 Four Patch Units.

C

Four Patch Unit Diagrams

6. Referring to *Block Assembly Diagrams* lay out 1 B square and 4 triangle-squares of 1 color and 4 Four Patch Units of another color. Join into rows; join rows to complete block. Make 40 blocks.

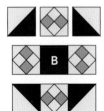

B

Block Assembly Diagrams

Quilt Assembly

1. Referring to *Sashing Diagram*, join 1 D sashing strip to left edge of block. Join 1 E square to end of 1 D sashing strip; add to top edge of block. Repeat for remaining blocks.

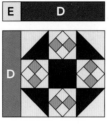

E D

D

Sashing Diagram

2. Referring to *Corner Unit Diagram*, join 2 setting triangles and 1 F sashing strip. Trim excess sashing at corner. Make 4 Corner Units.

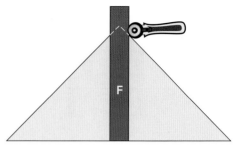

F

Corner Unit Diagram

3. Lay out blocks and remaining sashing strips, sashing squares, setting triangles and Corner Units as shown in *Quilt Top Assembly Diagram*.

4. Join into diagonal rows; join rows to complete quilt center.

5. Join 9 D sashing strips to make 1 border. Make 4 borders.

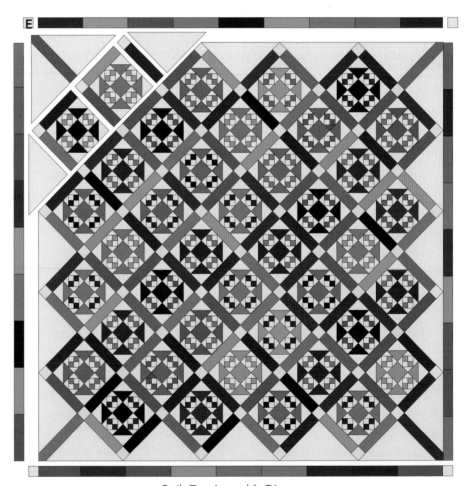

E

Quilt Top Assembly Diagram

6. Referring to *Quilt Top Assembly Diagram*, join 1 border to each side of quilt. Add 1 E sashing square to each end of remaining borders. Join to top and bottom of quilt.

Finishing

1. Divide backing into 3 (2½-yard) lengths. Cut 1 piece in half lengthwise to make 2 narrow panels. Sew 1 wide panel to each side of 1 narrow panel. Remaining piece is extra and can be used to make a hanging sleeve.

2. Layer backing, batting, and quilt top; baste. Quilt as desired. Quilt shown has circle and teardrop motifs in the blocks, pumpkin seeds in the sashing, and feather motifs in the setting triangles.

3. Join 2¼"-wide medium batik strips into 1 continuous piece for straight-grain French-fold binding. Add binding to quilt.

DESIGNER

A lifelong stitcher, Iowan Sandra Holmes has concentrated on quilting for the past 12 years. Retirement enables her to explore new techniques to make the traditional patterns she loves. ✳

TRIED & TRUE

The bright floral prints in this block are from the Potpourri collection by P & B Textiles.

Blue Bayou

Designer Toby Lischko combined traditional patchwork with contemporary fabrics to make this stunning batik quilt.

PROJECT RATING: INTERMEDIATE
Size: 99" × 99"
Blocks: 64 (10") blocks

MATERIALS

2½ yards navy batik
3¾ yards medium blue batik
1 yard white batik
1 yard medium blue print #1
1 yard medium blue print #2
1¼ yards medium blue print #3
1¼ yards medium blue print #4
3 yards light blue print #1
1 yard light blue print #2
9 yards backing fabric
King-size quilt batting

Cutting

Measurements include ¼" seam allowances. Border strips are exact length needed. You may want to make them longer to allow for piecing variations.

From navy batik, cut:

- 5 (2⅞"-wide) strips. From strips, cut 64 (2⅞") squares. Cut squares in half diagonally to make 128 half-square E triangles.
- 28 (2½"-wide) strips. From strips, cut 448 (2½") A squares.

From medium blue batik, cut:

- 11 (4½"-wide) strips. Piece strips to make 2 (4½" × 99½") top and bottom outer borders and 2 (4½" × 91½") side outer borders.
- 10 (2⅞"-wide) strips. From strips, cut 128 (2⅞") squares. Cut squares in half diagonally to make 256 half-square E triangles.
- 10 (2½"-wide) strips. Piece strips to make 2 (2½" × 84½") top and bottom inner borders and 2 (2½" × 80½") side inner borders.
- 11 (2¼"-wide) strips for binding.

From white batik, cut:

- 10 (2⅞"-wide) strips. From strips, cut 128 (2⅞") squares. Cut squares in half diagonally to make 256 half-square E triangles.

From medium blue print #1, cut:

- 3 (6½"-wide) strips. From strips, cut 16 (6½") B squares.

- 2 (4"-wide) strips. From strips, cut 6 (4" × 12") G rectangles.

From medium blue print #2, cut:

- 3 (6½"-wide) strips. From strips, cut 16 (6½") B squares.
- 2 (4"-wide) strips. From strips, cut 6 (4" × 12") G rectangles.

From medium blue print #3, cut:

- 2 (4⅞"-wide) strips. From strips, cut 16 (4⅞") squares. Cut squares in half diagonally to make 32 half-square F triangles.
- 2 (4"-wide) strips. From strips, cut 6 (4" × 12") G rectangles.
- 8 (2½"-wide) strips. From strips, cut 128 (2½") A squares.

From medium blue print #4, cut:

- 2 (4⅞"-wide) strips. From strips, cut 16 (4⅞") squares. Cut squares in half diagonally to make 32 half-square F triangles.
- 2 (4"-wide) strips. From strips, cut 6 (4" × 12") G rectangles.
- 8 (2½"-wide) strips. From strips, cut 128 (2½") A squares.

From light blue print #1, cut:

- 2 (4"-wide) strips. From strips, cut 6 (4" × 12") G rectangles.

- 38 (2½"-wide) strips. From strips, cut 128 (2½" × 6½") C rectangles and 128 (2½" × 4½") D rectangles.

From light blue print #2, cut:

- 2 (4"-wide) strips. From strips, cut 6 (4" × 12") G rectangles.
- 10 (2½"-wide) strips. From strips, cut 160 (2½") A squares.

Block 1 Assembly

1. Choose 4 navy A squares and 1 medium blue print #1 B square. Referring to *Center Unit 1 Assembly Diagrams*, place 1 A square atop 1 B square, right sides facing. Stitch diagonally from corner to corner as shown. Trim ¼" beyond stitching. Press open to reveal triangle. Repeat for 3 remaining corners to complete 1 Block 1 Center Unit. Make 16 Block 1 Center Units.

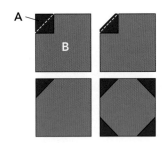

Center Unit 1 Assembly Diagrams

2. In the same manner, make 16 Block 1 Center Units using navy A squares and medium blue print #2 B squares.

3. Referring to *Unit 1 Assembly Diagrams*, place 1 navy A square atop 1 light blue print #1 C rectangle, right sides facing. Stitch diagonally from corner to corner as shown. Trim ¼" beyond stitching. Press open to reveal triangle. Repeat for opposite end of rectangle to complete 1 Unit 1. Make 128 Unit 1.

Unit 1 Assembly Diagrams

4. Join 1 white E triangle and 1 medium blue E triangle to make a triangle-square *(Triangle-Square Diagrams)*. Make 128 white/medium blue triangle-squares.

Triangle-Square Diagrams

5. Referring to *Block 1 Assembly Diagram*, lay out 1 Block 1 Center Unit, 4 Unit 1, and 4 white/medium blue triangle-squares. Join into rows; join rows to complete 1 Block 1 *(Block 1 Diagram)*. Make 32 Block 1.

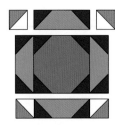

Block 1 Assembly Diagram

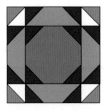

Block 1 Diagram

Block 2 Assembly

1. Join 1 white E triangle and 1 navy E triangle to make 1 white/navy triangle-square *(Triangle-Square Diagrams)*. Make 128 white/navy triangle-squares.

2. Referring to *Flying Geese Unit Assembly Diagrams*, place 1 medium blue print #3 A square atop 1 light blue print #1 D rectangle, right

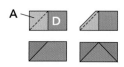

Flying Geese Unit Assembly Diagrams

sides facing. Stitch diagonally from corner to corner as shown. Trim ¼" beyond stitching. Press open to reveal triangle. Repeat for opposite end of rectangle to complete 1 Flying Geese Unit. Make 64 Flying Geese Units.

3. In the same manner, make 64 Flying Geese Units using medium blue print #4 A squares and light blue print #1 D rectangles.

4. Lay out 3 light blue print #2 A squares, 4 medium blue E triangles, 1 medium blue print #3 F triangle, and 1 medium blue print #4 F triangle. Join pieces as shown in *Center Unit 2 Assembly Diagrams* to make 1 Block 2 Center Unit. Make 32 Block 2 Center Units.

Center Unit 2 Assembly Diagrams

5. Referring to *Block 2 Assembly Diagram*, lay out 1 Block 2 Center Unit, 4 Flying Geese Units, 4 navy/white triangle-squares, 2 navy A squares, and 2 light blue print #2 A squares. Join into horizontal rows; join rows to complete 1 Block 2 *(Block 2 Diagram)*. Make 32 Block 2.

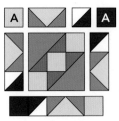 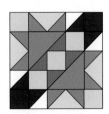

Block 2 Assembly Diagram   Block 2 Diagram

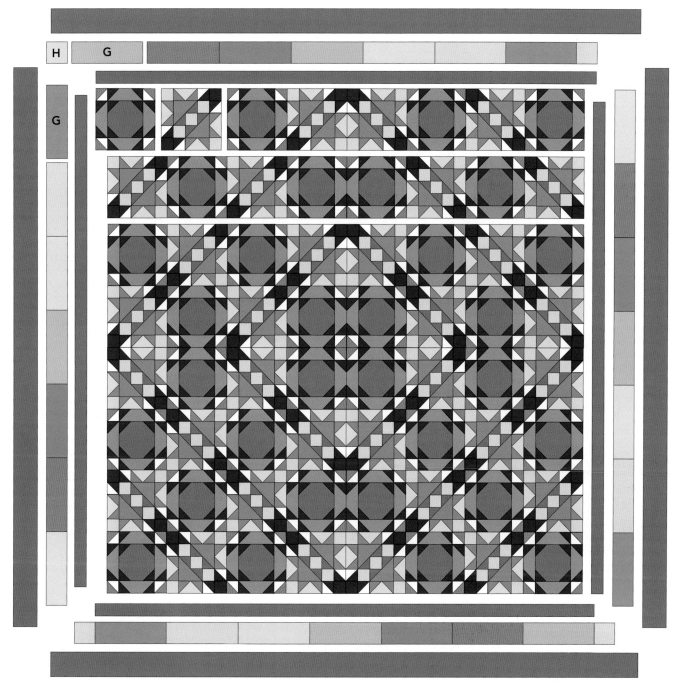

Quilt Top Assembly Diagram

Quilt Assembly

1. Lay out blocks as shown in *Quilt Top Assembly Diagram*. Join into rows; join rows to complete quilt center.

2. Join G border rectangles to make 1 continuous strip. From strips, cut 2 (4" × 91½") top and bottom middle borders and 2 (4" × 84½") side middle borders.

3. Add side inner borders to quilt center. Add top and bottom inner borders to quilt. Repeat for pieced middle borders and outer borders.

Finishing

1. Divide backing fabric into 3 (3-yard) lengths. Join panels lengthwise.

2. Layer backing, batting, and quilt top; baste. Quilt as desired. Quilt shown is quilted with an allover design *(Quilting Diagram on page 40)*.

3. Join 2¼"-wide medium blue solid strips into 1 continuous piece for straight-grain French-fold binding. Add binding to quilt.

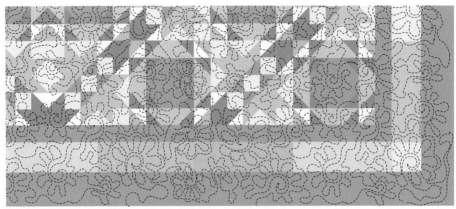

Quilting Diagram

Create a wallhanging using reproduction prints such as the Elizabeth c. 1860–1900 collection by Nancy Gere for Windham Fabrics.

Wallhanging (40" × 40")

Blocks	16 (10") blocks

MATERIALS

Light Red Print	⅜ yard
Medium Red Print	⅝ yard
Dark Red Print	⅜ yard
Black Print	¾ yard
Brown Print	⅝ yard
Beige Print	⅜ yard
Binding	⅜ yard
Backing Fabric	2½ yards
Batting	Crib-size

CUTTING

Light Red Print	16 A squares
	32 D rectangles
Medium Red Print	64 A squares
	32 half-square E triangles
	16 half-square F triangles
Dark Red Print	8 B squares
Black Print	112 A squares
	64 half-square E triangles
Brown Print	24 A squares
	32 C rectangles
Beige Print	64 half-square E triangles
Binding	5 (2¼"-wide) strips

DESIGNER

Toby Lischko is a teacher, pattern designer, and award-winning quilter. She's been quilting since 1985, and teaching quilting workshops since 1995. Toby loves to travel and teach and hopes to instill passion for quilting in others. ✳

QUILT BY **Marianne Fons**.
MACHINE QUILTED BY **LuAnn Downs**.

Crossed Kayaks

Marianne Fons combined batik fabrics, the traditional Crossed Canoes block, and a shaded layout to create her contemporary quilt. She says, "This quilt will benefit my sister-in-law Valerie Fons, now a cancer survivor, who paddled more than 30,000 miles during her career as a long-distance kayaker."

PROJECT RATING: INTERMEDIATE

Size: 96" × 96"

Blocks: 36 (12") Crossed Canoes blocks

MATERIALS

⅝ yard each light blue and light green batik

1¼ yards medium blue batik

1½ yards medium green batik

1¾ yards each dark blue and dark green batik

4¾ yards navy batik

⅜ yard dark pink batik

Crossed Kayaks Template Set (optional)

8⅝ yards backing fabric

King-size quilt batting

Cutting

Measurements include ¼" seam allowances. Patterns for A, B, and C are on page 47.

From each light blue and light green batik, cut:

- 1 (6⅞"-wide) strip. From strip, cut 8 A triangles and 8 A triangles reversed.
- 1 (8"-wide) strip. From strip, cut 8 B triangles.
- 1 (2⅞"-wide) strip. From strip, cut 4 (2⅞") squares. Cut squares in half diagonally to make 8 half-square D triangles.

From each medium blue and medium green batik, cut:

- 3 (6⅞"-wide) strips. From strips, cut 24 A triangles and 24 A triangles reversed.
- 2 (8"-wide) strips. From strips, cut 24 B triangles.
- 1 (2⅞"-wide) strip. From strip, cut 12 (2⅞") squares. Cut squares in half diagonally to make 24 half-square D triangles.

From medium green batik, cut:

- 2 (5½"-wide) strips. From strips, cut 28 C triangles.

From each dark blue and dark green batik, cut:

- 5 (6⅞"-wide) strips. From strips, cut 40 A triangles and 40 A triangles reversed.
- 2 (8"-wide) strips. From strips, cut 40 B triangles.
- 2 (2⅞"-wide) strips. From strips, cut 20 (2⅞") squares. Cut squares in half diagonally to make 40 half-square D triangles.

From navy batik, cut:

- 4 (14½"-wide) strips. From strips, cut 24 (14½" × 5½") E rectangles.
- 6 (12½"-wide) strips. From strips, cut 84 (12½" × 2½") sashing rectangles.
- 1 (6½"-wide) strip. From strip, cut 4 (6½") F squares.
- 11 (2¼"-wide) strips for binding.

From dark pink batik, cut:

- 4 (2½"-wide) strips. From strips, cut 49 (2½") sashing squares.

Block Assembly

1. Join 1 light green A triangle, 1 light green A triangle reversed, 1 light blue B triangle, and 1 light green D triangle as shown in *Block Unit Diagrams*. Make 8 light green block units.

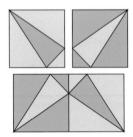

MAKE 8   **MAKE 8**

Block Unit Diagrams

2. In the same manner, make 8 block units using 1 light blue A triangle, 1 light blue A triangle reversed, 1 light green B triangle, and 1 light blue D triangle in each.

3. Lay out block units as shown in *Block Assembly Diagram*. Join into rows; join rows to complete 1 light block (*Block Diagrams*). Make 4 light blocks.

Block Assembly Diagram

4. In the same manner, make 12 medium blocks using medium blue and medium green A, B, and D triangles. Make 20 dark blocks using dark blue and dark green A, B, and D triangles.

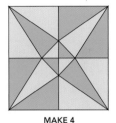
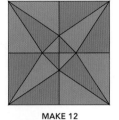

MAKE 4   **MAKE 12**

MAKE 20

Block Diagrams

Border Assembly

1. Place B template atop 1 navy E rectangle, aligning top edges and placing point of template exactly at corner of strip as shown in *Trimming Diagrams*. Trim outer slanted edge. Repeat for opposite end of rectangle to make 1 border unit. Make 24 border units.

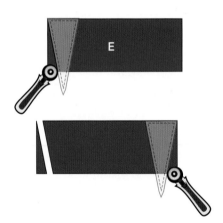

Trimming Diagrams

2. Place B template atop 1 navy F square, aligning right side edges and placing corner of template exactly at upper right corner of square as shown in *Corner Unit Diagrams*. Draw a line along top edge of template.

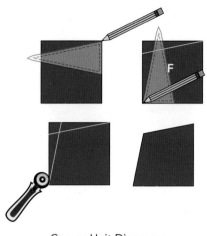

Corner Unit Diagrams

3. Place B template atop navy F square, aligning bottom edges and placing corner of template exactly at lower left corner of square as shown. Draw a line along left edge of template.

4. Cut on drawn lines to make 1 Corner Unit. Make 4 Corner Units.

5. Referring to *Quilt Top Assembly Diagram* on page 45, join 6 border units and 7 medium green C triangles to complete 1 border. Make 4 borders.

Quilt Assembly

1. Lay out blocks, navy sashing rectangles, and dark pink sashing squares as shown in *Quilt Top Assembly Diagram*.

2. Join into rows; join rows to complete quilt center.

3. Add 1 border to each side of quilt.

4. Join 1 corner unit to each end of remaining borders. Add borders to top and bottom of quilt.

Finishing

1. Divide backing into 3 (2⅞-yard) lengths. Join panels lengthwise.

2. Layer backing, batting, and quilt top; baste. Quilt as desired. Quilt shown was quilted in the ditch and with chains of small circles (*Quilting Diagram* on page 45).

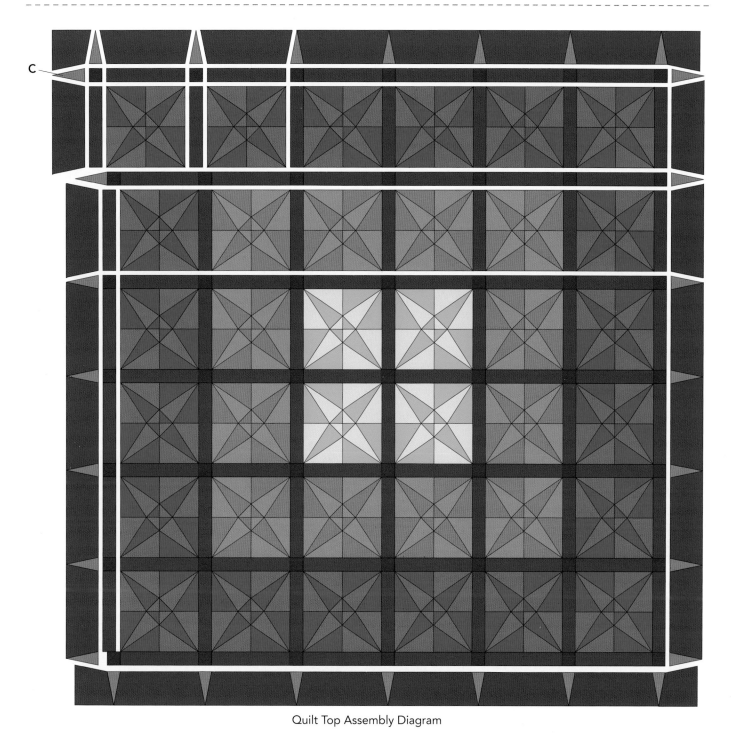

C

Quilt Top Assembly Diagram

3. Join 2¼"-wide navy strips into 1 continuous piece for straight-grain French-fold binding. Add binding to quilt.

Quilting Diagram

TRIED & TRUE

We made our block in traditional prints from the
Devon Shirtings collection by Nancy Gere for
Windham Fabrics. ✳

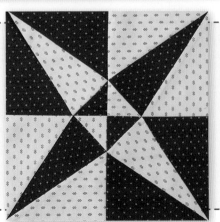

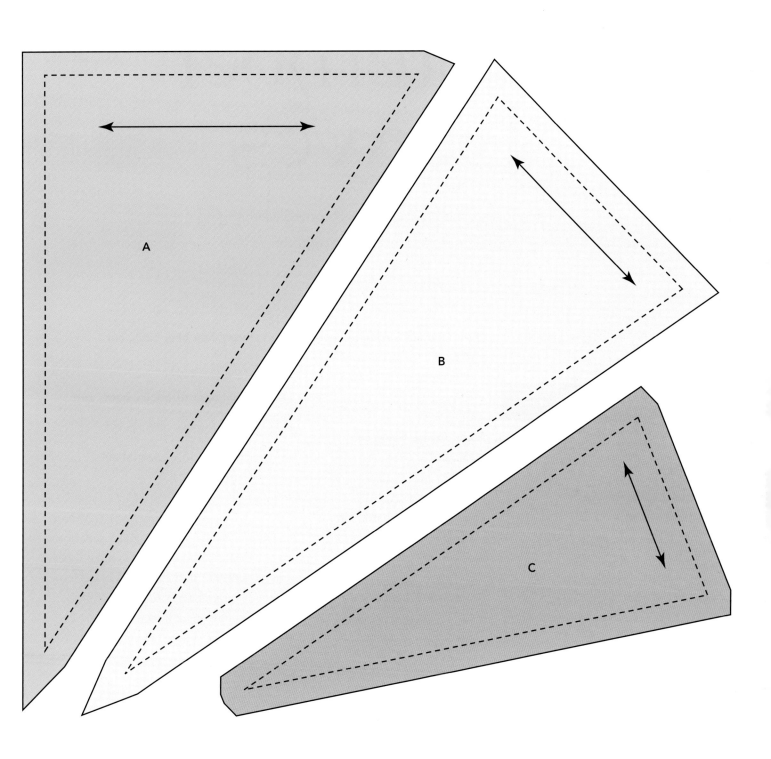

A

B

C

September Leaves

Challenge yourself to make this stunning wallhanging!

Curved seams and batik fabrics create an undulating pattern in this gorgeous seasonal quilt.

PROJECT RATING: CHALLENGING

Size: 42" × 42"

MATERIALS

1 yard medium turquoise batik

¾ yard orange batik

¾ yard black-grid batik

¾ yard dark brown print

¾ yard rust stripe

½ yard tan batik

¼ yard dark blue batik

⅜ yard dark turquoise batik for binding

7¾ yards multi-colored purchased trim or yarn (optional)

Template material

2¾ yards backing fabric

Crib-size quilt batting

Cutting

Make templates for the patterns on pages 52–53. Punch holes in templates at points indicated by dots on pattern pieces. Measurements include ¼" seam allowances.

From medium turquoise batik, cut:

• 12 B.

• 12 B reversed.

• 4 D.

• 4 D reversed.

From orange batik, cut:

• 4 A.

• 8 B.

• 8 B reversed.

From black-grid batik, cut:

• 12 A.

• 2 C.

• 2 C reversed.

From dark brown print, cut:

• 4 A.

• 4 B.

• 4 B reversed.

• 2 C.

• 2 C reversed.

From rust stripe, cut:

• 12 B.

• 12 B reversed.

From tan batik, cut:

• 4 A.

• 4 B.

• 4 B reversed.

From dark blue batik, cut:

• 4 B.

• 4 B reversed.

From dark turquoise batik, cut:

• 5 (2¼"-wide) strips for binding.

Pieced Half Clamshell Unit Assembly

1. Referring to *Pieced Half Clamshell Unit Diagrams* and *Sew Easy: Clamshell Units* on page 54, join 1 dark brown C and 1 turquoise D to make 1 Pieced Half Clamshell Unit. Make 2 brown/turquoise Pieced Half Clamshell Units and 2 brown/turquoise Pieced Half Clamshell Units reverse.

Pieced Half Clamshell Unit Diagrams

Quilt Top Assembly Diagram

2. In the same manner, join 1 black grid C and 1 turquoise D to make 1 Pieced Half Clamshell Unit. Make 2 black/turquoise Pieced Half Clamshell Units and 2 black/turquoise Pieced Half Clamshell Units reversed.

Quilt Top Assembly

1. Referring to *Quilt Top Assembly Diagram*, and photo on page 51, lay out clamshells, half clamshells, and Pieced Half Clamshell Units as shown.

2. Referring to *Sew Easy: Clamshell Units* on page 54, join into diagonal rows, stitching from dot to dot, and leaving seam allowances free beyond dots. If desired, sew straight seams between Half Clamshells before stitching curved seams.

3. In the same manner, join rows to complete quilt center.

Finishing

1. Divide backing fabric into 2 (1⅜-yard) pieces. Cut one piece in half length-wise. Join 1 narrow panel to wider panel. Remaining panel is extra and may be used to make a hanging sleeve.

2. Layer backing, batting, and quilt top; baste. Quilt as desired. Quilt shown was quilted with a freehand swirl design *(Quilting Diagram)*.

3. Join 2¼"-wide dark turquoise batik strips into 1 continuous piece for straight-grain French-fold binding. Add binding to quilt.

4. If desired, stitch purchased trim to quilt as shown in photo on page 51.

Quilting Diagram

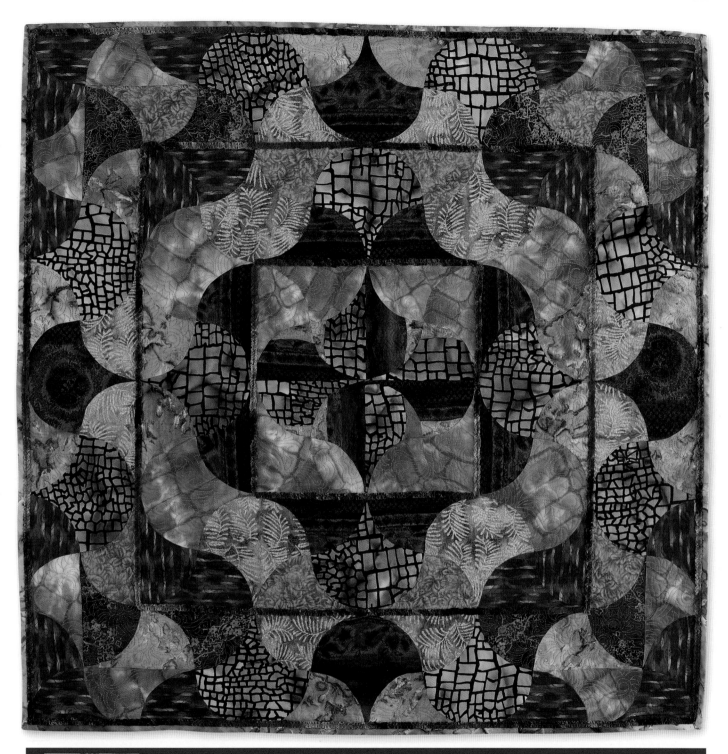

DESIGNER

Award–winning quilter and teacher Marilyn Badger has been a frequent guest on "Fons & Porter's Love of Quilting" on public television. In addition to teaching classes at home and abroad, she serves as a consultant to American Professional Quilting Systems.

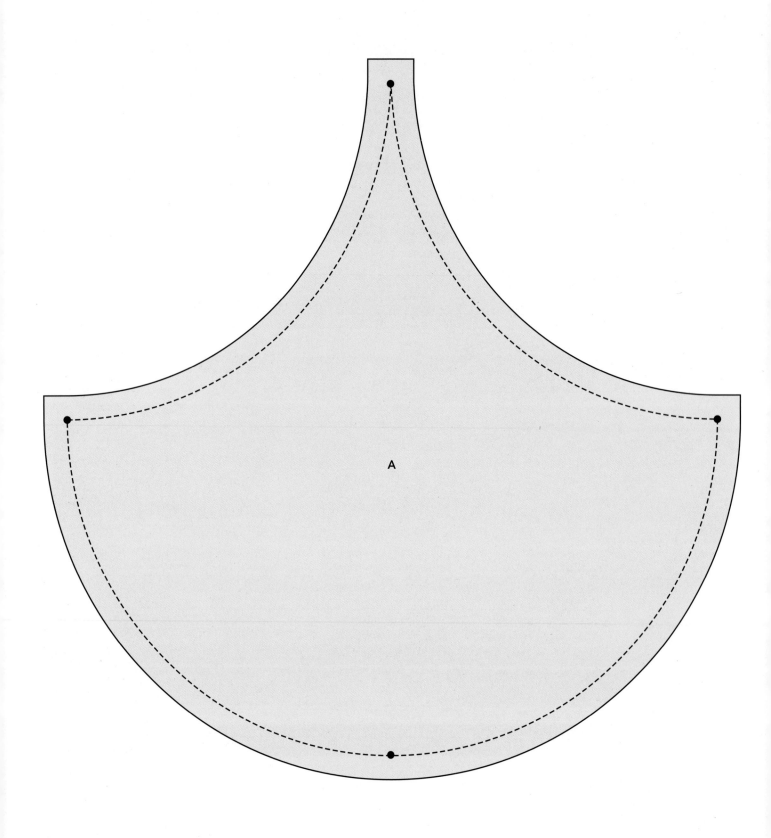

A

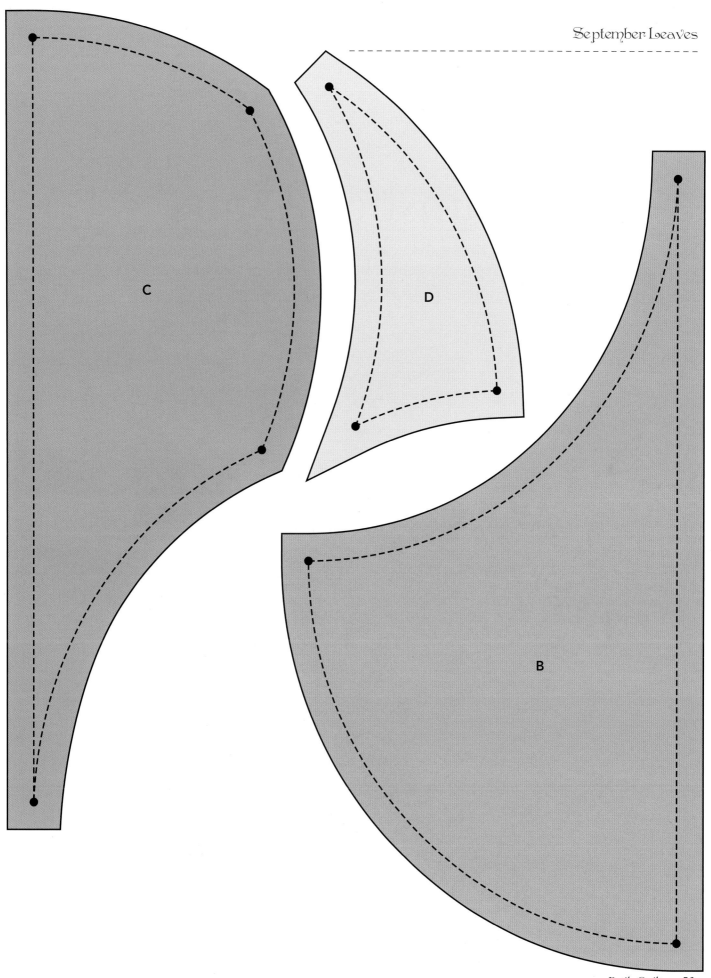

Sew Easy™

Clamshell Units

To sew clamshell units for *September Leaves*, follow these simple steps.

Pieced Half Clamshell Units

1. Mark dots on wrong side of fabric pieces C and D at seam-line intersections as indicated on patterns. Lay out C and D pieces as shown in *Photo A*.

2. With right sides together, align pieces by sticking a pin through dot on D piece and out through dot on C piece (*Photo B*). Pin pieces together at dots.

3. With D piece on top, join pieces, adjusting curve and keeping raw edges aligned as you sew (*Photo C*).

4. Press seam allowance toward C to complete Pieced Half Clamshell Unit (*Photo D*).

A

B

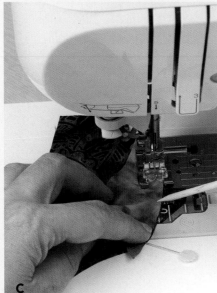

C

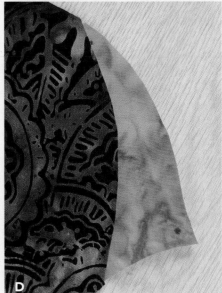

D

E

F

Joining Clamshell Units

1. Mark dots on A and B pieces and align with pins as before. Place concave edge of B piece on top of convex edge of A piece; join pieces, aligning edges as you sew *(Photo E)*.

2. Referring to *Quilt Top Assembly Diagram* on page 50, add Clamshell Units to make diagonal rows *(Photo F)*.

QUILT BY **Tammy Silvers and Julie LaBauve**.
MACHINE QUILTED BY **Stitch'n Quilt**.

Woven Wonder

You'll be amazed at how quick and easy it is to make this
wonderful quilt, designed with strip sets.

PROJECT RATING: EASY
Size: 53" × 68"
Blocks: 12 (15") blocks

MATERIALS

1¼ yards red batik
1¼ yards blue batik
1¾ yards orange batik
¾ yard yellow batik
1⅛ yards purple batik
3½ yards backing fabric
Twin-size quilt batting

Cutting

Measurements include ¼" seam
allowances. Border strips are exact
length needed. You may want to make
them longer to allow for piecing
variations.

From red batik, cut:

- 3 (8"-wide) strips for strip sets.
- 3 (3½"-wide) strips for strip sets.
- 2 (2"-wide) strips for strip sets.

From blue batik, cut:

- 2 (8"-wide) strips for strip sets.
- 2 (3½"-wide) strips for strip sets.

- 2 (2"-wide) strips for strip sets.
- 7 (1½"-wide) strips. From strips, cut
  8 (1½" × 3½") F rectangles. Piece remaining strips to make 2 (1½" × 60½")
  side inner borders and 2 (1½" × 45½")
  top and bottom inner borders.

From orange batik, cut:

- 3 (8"-wide) strips for strip sets.
- 3 (3½"-wide) strips for strip sets.
- 7 (2¼"-wide) strips for binding.
- 2 (2"-wide) strips for strip sets.

From yellow batik, cut:

- 12 (2"-wide) strips for strip sets.

From purple batik, cut:

- 6 (3½"-wide) strips. From strips, cut 4
  (3½") D squares. Piece remaining strips
  to make 2 (3½" × 60½") side outer borders
  and 2 (3½" × 45½") top and bottom
  outer borders.
- 6 (2"-wide) strips for strip sets.
- 1 (1½"-wide) strip. From strip, cut 4
  (1½") E squares.

Block Assembly

1. Join 1 (8"-wide) red strip, 2 (2"-wide)
yellow strips, 1 (2"-wide) purple strip,
and 1 (3½"-wide) red strip as shown
in *Strip Set #1 Diagram*. Make 3 Strip
Set #1. From strip sets, cut 6 (8"-wide)
segment A, 6 (3½"-wide) segment B,
and 6 (2"-wide) segment C.

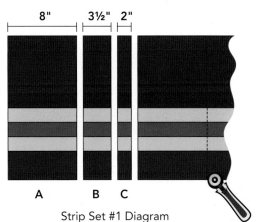

Strip Set #1 Diagram

2. Join 1 (8"-wide) orange strip, 2 (2"-wide)
yellow strips, 1 (2"-wide) purple strip,
and 1 (3½"-wide) orange strip as shown
in *Strip Set #2 Diagram*. Make 3 Strip Set
#2. From strip sets, cut 6 (8"-wide)
segment A, 6 (3½"-wide) segment B,
and 6 (2"-wide) segment C.

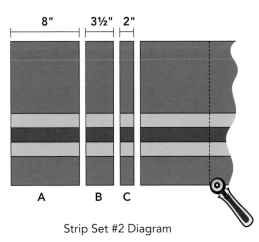

Strip Set #2 Diagram

3. Join 1 (8"-wide) blue strip, 2 (2"-wide) red strips, 1 (2"-wide) blue strip, and 1 (3½"-wide) blue strip as shown in *Strip Set #3 Diagram*. From strip set, cut 12 (2"-wide) segment C.

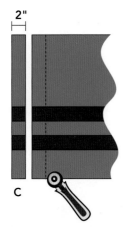

Strip Set #3 Diagram

4. Join 1 (8"-wide) blue strip, 2 (2"-wide) orange strips, 1 (2"-wide) blue strip, and 1 (3½"-wide) blue strip as shown in *Strip Set #4 Diagram*. From strip set, cut 12 (2"-wide) segment C.

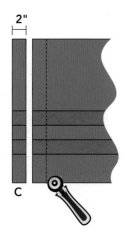

Strip Set #4 Diagram

5. Lay out 1 segment A, 3 segment C, and 1 segment B as shown in *Block Assembly Diagram*. Join segments to complete 1 block *(Block Diagrams)*. Make 12 blocks in colors as shown.

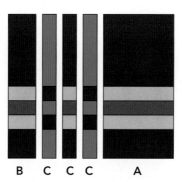

B C C C A

Block Assembly Diagram

MAKE 3

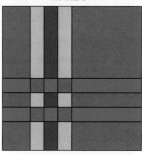

MAKE 3

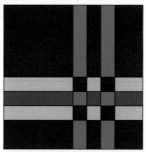

MAKE 3

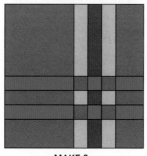

MAKE 3

Block Diagrams

Quilt Assembly

1. Lay out blocks as shown in *Quilt Top Assembly Diagram* on page 59. Join blocks into rows; join rows to complete quilt center.

2. Join 1 blue side inner border and 1 purple outer border to make 1 side border. Make 2 side borders.

3. In the same manner, make top and bottom borders.

4. Join 1 purple D square, 1 purple E square, and 2 blue F rectangles as shown in *Corner Unit Diagrams*. Make 4 Corner Units.

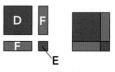

Corner Unit Diagrams

5. Add side borders to quilt center.

6. Add 1 Corner Unit to each end of top and bottom borders. Add borders to quilt.

Finishing

1. Divide backing into 2 (1¾-yard) lengths. Join panels lengthwise. Seam will run horizontally.

2. Layer backing, batting, and quilt top; baste. Quilt as desired. Quilt shown was quilted with an allover cloud design *(Quilting Diagram on page 59)*.

3. Join 2¼"-wide orange strips into 1 continuous piece for straight-grain French-fold binding. Add binding to quilt.

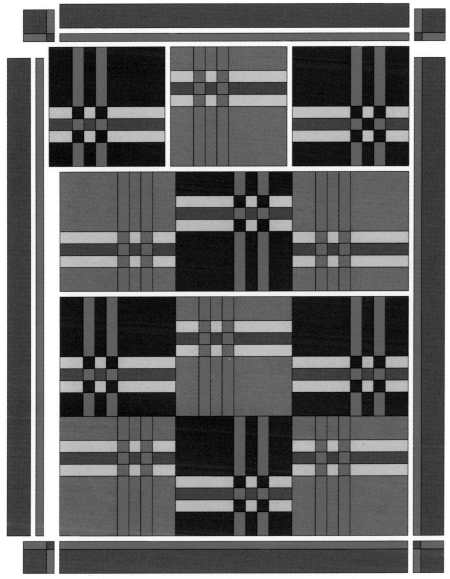

Quilt Top Assembly Diagram

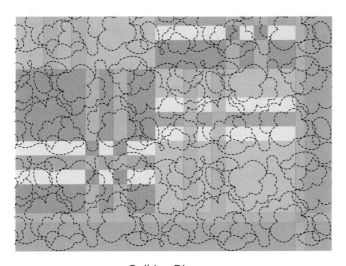

Quilting Diagram

DESIGNERS

Tammy Silvers and Julia LaBauve started Outside the Line Designs in 2006, after several years of friendship and quilting. As a team they have designed many quilts that play off of their combined interests and strengths, as well as their mutual love of vibrant fabric and strong graphic design. They are authors of the AQS book *Small Quilts, Big Events*. ✳

TRIED & TRUE

We made our block with seashore-motif prints. The fabric collection is Seashells by Exclusively Quilters.

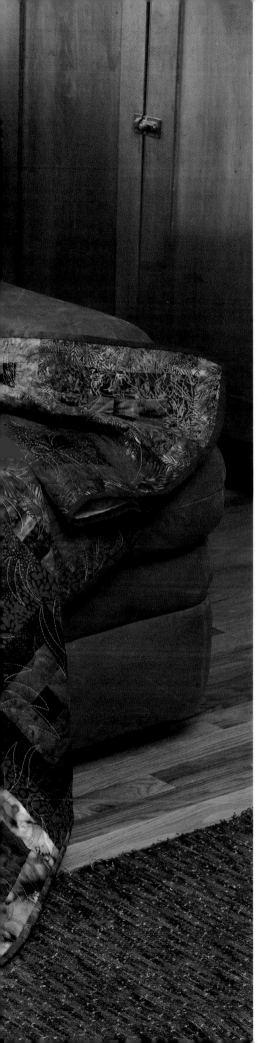

QUILT BY **Lori Christianson.**

On the Dark Side

Designer Lori Christianson created a Courthouse Steps Log Cabin variation that uses each fabric on all four sides instead of alternating dark and light value fabrics on opposite sides of a center square. The repeat fabrics—dramatic medium and dark batiks—form bold squares in this contemporary quilt.

PROJECT RATING: EASY

Size: 73½" × 84"

Blocks: 56 (10½") Log Cabin blocks

MATERIALS

28 fat quarters★ assorted medium/
 dark batiks for blocks

1 fat quarter★ black print for block
 centers

¾ yard dark batik for binding

5 yards backing fabric

Twin-Size batting

★fat quarter = 18" × 20"

Cutting

Measurements include ¼" seam allowances.

From each fat quarter, cut:

• 8 (2"-wide) strips. From strips, cut:
  • 4 (2" × 11") #4 pieces.
  • 8 (2" × 8") #3 pieces.
  • 8 (2" × 5") #2 pieces.
  • 4 (2" × 2") #1 pieces.

From black fat quarter, cut:

• 6 (2"-wide) strips. From strips, cut 56
  (2") center squares.

From dark batik, cut:

• 9 (2¼"-wide) strips for binding.

Batik Quilts 61

Block Assembly

1. Lay out pieces as shown in *Block Assembly Diagram*.

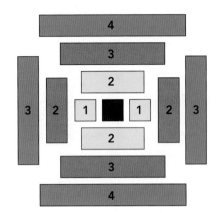

Block Assembly Diagram

2. Join strips in numerical order to complete 1 Log Cabin block *(Block Diagram)*. Make 56 blocks.

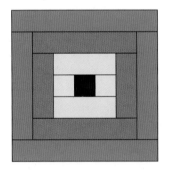

Block Diagram

Quilt Assembly

1. Lay out blocks as shown in *Quilt Top Assembly Diagram*.

2. Join blocks into rows; join rows to complete quilt top.

Finishing

1. Divide backing into 2 (2½-yard) lengths. Divide 1 panel in half lengthwise. Join 1 narrow panel to each side of wide panel. Press seam allowances toward narrow panels.

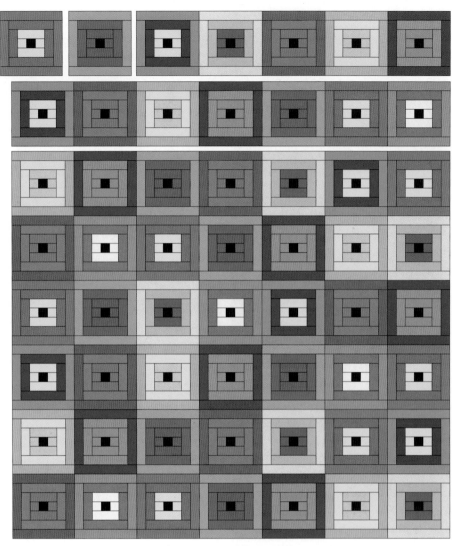

Quilt Top Assembly Diagram

2. Layer backing, batting, and quilt top; baste. Quilt as desired. Quilt shown was machine quilted with a meandering swirling leaf pattern.

3. Join 2¼" dark batik strips into 1 continuous piece for straight-grain French-fold binding. Add binding to quilt.

TRIED & TRUE

Our version uses a collection of 1930s reproduction fabrics. ✳

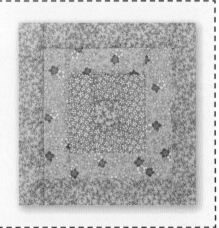

Tucson Sunset

Liz Porter dipped into her vast stash of batiks to make a quilt that depicts the colors of dusk in her favorite Arizona city.

PROJECT RATING: INTERMEDIATE

Size: 107" × 107"

Blocks: 36 (15") Star blocks

MATERIALS

⅜ yard each of 36 assorted batik prints

½ yard gold batik print for inner border

3½ yards brown batik print for outer border and binding

Marti Michell's Peaky and Spike Template Set R or template material

9¾ yards backing fabric

King-size quilt batting

Cutting

Measurements include ¼" seam allowances. Border strips are exact length needed. You may want to make them longer to allow for piecing variations. Patterns for B and C triangles are on page 67.

From each batik print, cut:

• 1 (5½"-wide) strip. From strip, cut 5 (5½") A squares.

• 1 (5¾"-wide) strip. From strip, cut 4 B triangles, 4 C triangles, and 4 C triangles reversed.

From gold batik print, cut:

• 10 (1½"-wide) strips. Piece strips to make 2 (1½" × 92½") top and bottom inner borders and 2 (1½" × 90½") side inner borders.

From brown batik print, cut:

• 11 (8"-wide) strips. Piece strips to make 2 (8" × 107½") top and bottom inner borders and 2 (8" × 92½") side inner borders.

• 12 (2¼"-wide) strips for binding.

Block Assembly

1. Choose 4 matching A squares and 4 B triangles for block background and 4 matching C triangles, 4 C triangles reversed, and 1 A square for star.

2. Join 1 B triangle, 1 C triangle, and 1 C triangle reversed as shown in *Star Point Unit Diagrams*. Make 4 Star Point Units.

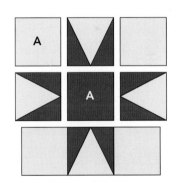

Star Point Unit Diagrams

3. Lay out A squares and Star Point Units as shown in *Block Assembly Diagram*. Join into rows; join rows to complete 1 block *(Block Diagram)*. Make 36 blocks.

Block Assembly Diagram

Block Diagram

Quilt Assembly

1. Lay out blocks as shown in *Quilt Top Assembly Diagram*. Join into rows; join rows to complete quilt center.

2. Add gold batik print side inner borders to quilt center. Add top and bottom inner borders to quilt.

3. Repeat for brown batik print outer borders.

Finishing

1. Divide backing into 3 (3¼-yard) lengths. Join panels lengthwise.

2. Layer backing, batting, and quilt top; baste. Quilt as desired. Quilt shown was quilted with an allover plume design *(Quilting Diagram)*.

3. Join 2¼"-wide brown batik print strips into 1 continuous piece for straight-grain French-fold binding. Add binding to quilt.

Quilt Top Assembly Diagram

Quilting Diagram

TRIED & TRUE

Choose two favorite prints such as the ones we used for our version. Fabrics are from the Tweet Others with Kindness collection by Kelly Mueller of the Wooden Bear for Red Rooster Fabrics.

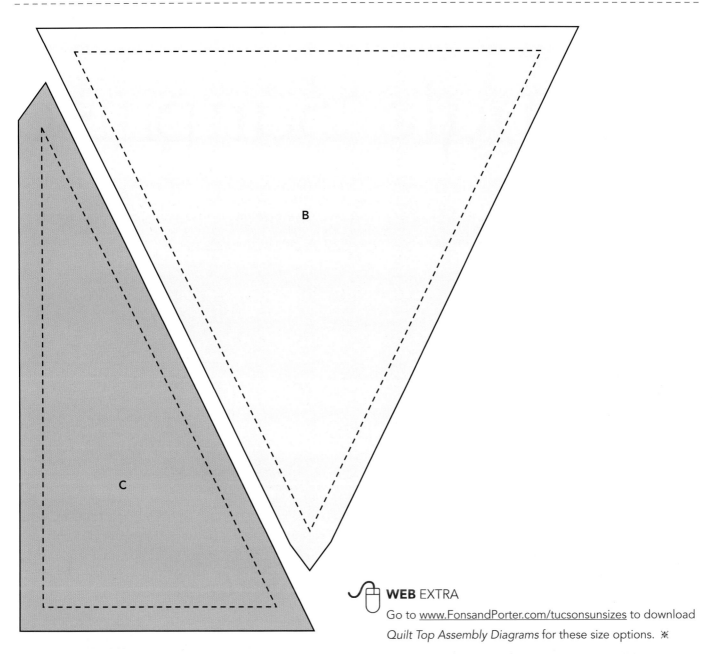

WEB EXTRA

Go to www.FonsandPorter.com/tucsonsunsizes to download

Quilt Top Assembly Diagrams for these size options. ✳

SIZE OPTIONS

	Throw (62" × 77")	Full (77" × 92")	Queen (92" × 92")
Blocks	12	20	25
Setting	3 × 4	4 × 5	5 × 5

MATERIALS

	Throw (62" × 77")	Full (77" × 92")	Queen (92" × 92")
Assorted Batik Prints	⅜ yard each of 12	⅜ yard each of 20	⅜ yard each of 25
Gold Batik Print	⅜ yard	½ yard	½ yard
Brown Batik Print	2¼ yards	2⅝ yards	2¾ yards
Backing Fabric	4 yards	5½ yards	8¼ yards
Batting	Twin-size	Full-size	King-size

Triangle Surprise

What a great way to use scraps! Designer Edyta Sitar used batiks, homespuns, reproductions, shirtings, and contemporary prints all together in this appealing quilt.

PROJECT RATING: EASY

Size: 56" × 56"

Blocks: 49 (8") blocks

MATERIALS

17 fat quarters★ assorted light prints

17 fat quarters★ assorted dark prints

½ yard teal print for binding

8 Laundry Basket Quilts Half-Square Triangle Exchange Papers (optional)

3½ yards backing fabric

Twin-size quilt batting

★fat quarter = 18" × 20"

Cutting

Measurements include ¼" seam allowances. Border strips are exact length needed. You may want to make them longer to allow for piecing variations.

NOTE: Instructions are written using Half-Square Triangle Exchange Paper cut into smaller sections. This will make more combinations of prints for a scrappier look. If not using these papers, make 2" finished triangle-squares using your preferred method.

From each light fat quarter, cut:

• 1 (6⅛"-wide) strip. From strip, cut 3 (6⅛") B squares.

• 1 (2⅞"-wide) strip. From strip, cut 6 (2⅞") squares. Cut squares in half diagonally to make 12 half-square A triangles.

From each dark fat quarter, cut:

• 1 (6⅛"-wide) strip. From strip, cut 3 (6⅛") B squares.

• 1 (2⅞"-wide) strips. From strips, cut 6 (2⅞") squares. Cut squares in half diagonally to make 12 half-square A triangles.

From teal print, cut:

• 7 (2¼"-wide) strips for binding.

Block Assembly

1. Cut triangle papers into 25 sections of 4 squares each. Layer 1 light print B square atop 1 dark print B square, right sides facing. Place 1 paper square atop pair of squares; pin in place.

2. Stitch on dashed lines as shown in *Stitching Diagram*. Cut on all solid lines, including outer lines, to make 8 triangle-squares. With paper still attached, press seam allowances of triangle-squares toward dark fabric. Repeat to make a total of 196 triangle-squares. Carefully remove paper from triangle-squares.

Stitching Diagram

3. Join 1 triangle-square and 2 dark print A triangles as shown in *Corner Unit Diagrams* on page 70. Make 100 dark Corner Units.

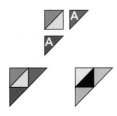

Corner Unit Diagrams

Dark Block Diagram

Quilt Assembly

1. Lay out blocks as shown in *Quilt Top Assembly Diagram*.

2. Join into rows; join rows to complete quilt top.

Finishing

1. Divide backing into 2 (1¾-yard) lengths. Cut 1 piece in half lengthwise to make 2 narrow panels. Join 1 narrow panel to wider panel; press seam allowances toward narrow panel. Remaining panel is extra and can be used to make a hanging sleeve.

2. Layer backing, batting, and quilt top; baste. Quilt as desired. Quilt shown was quilted with an allover design *(Quilting Diagram)*.

3. Join 2¼"-wide teal print strips into 1 continuous piece for straight-grain French-fold binding. Add binding to quilt.

Quilting Diagram

4. In the same manner, join 1 triangle-square and 2 light print A triangles to complete 1 light Corner Unit. Make 96 light Corner Units.

5. Lay out 4 dark Corner Units and 1 light print B square as shown in *Light Block Assembly Diagram*. Join to complete 1 light block *(Light Block Diagram)*. Make 25 light blocks.

Light Block Assembly Diagram

Light Block Diagram

6. Referring to *Dark Block Assembly Diagram*, join 4 light Corner Units and 1 dark print B square to complete 1 dark block *(Dark Block Diagram)*. Make 24 dark blocks.

Dark Block Assembly Diagram

Quilt Top Assembly Diagram

SIZE OPTIONS

	Twin (72" × 88")	Full (80" × 88")	Queen (88" × 104")
Blocks	99	110	143
Setting	9 × 11	10 × 11	11 × 13

MATERIALS

Assorted Light Prints	22 fat quarters	25 fat quarters	32 fat quarters
Assorted Dark Prints	22 fat quarters	25 fat quarters	32 fat quarters
Teal Print	¾ yard	¾ yard	⅞ yard
Backing Fabric	5¼ yards	7½ yards	8 yards
Batting	Twin-size	Full-size	Queen-size

 Go to www.FonsandPorter.com/jftrisprsizes to download *Quilt Top Assembly Diagrams* for these size options. ✳

DESIGNER

Edyta credits her family for her love of quilting and constant inspiration. As a designer for Moda, she shares her fabrics, quilts, and experiences with enthusiastic audiences worldwide. See more of Edyta's wonderful quilts in her book *Friendship Triangles*, published by Landauer Publishing.

Tranquility

Make this serene quilt using traditional blocks and a collection of color-coordinated batiks.

PROJECT RATING: EASY

Size: 65" × 65"

Blocks: 25 (10") blocks

MATERIALS

8 fat quarters★ assorted dark batik fabrics in brown, red, rust, and purple

2 yards tan batik for blocks

1 yard green batik for blocks and inner border

1¾ yards rust batik for outer border and binding

Fons & Porter Half & Quarter ruler (optional)

4 yards backing fabric

Twin-size quilt batting

★fat quarter = 18" × 20"

Cutting

Measurements include ¼" seam allowances. Border strips are exact length needed. You may want to make them longer to allow for piecing variations. Instructions are written for using the Fons & Porter Half & Quarter Ruler. For instructions on using this ruler, go to www.FonsandPorter.com/chst. If not using this ruler, follow cutting **NOTES**.

From each fat quarter, cut:

• 5 (3"-wide) strips. From strips, cut 10 (3") A squares and 28 half-square B triangles.

NOTE: If not using the Fons & Porter Half & Quarter Ruler, cut:

• 3 (3⅜"-wide) strips. From strips, cut 14 (3⅜") squares. Cut squares in half diagonally to make 28 half-square B triangles.

• 2 (3"-wide) strips. From strips, cut 10 (3") A squares.

From tan batik, cut:

• 2 (5½"-wide) strips. From strips, cut 13 (5½") C squares.

• 18 (3"-wide) strips. From strips, cut 48 (3") A squares and 276 half-square B triangles.

NOTE: If not using the Fons & Porter Half & Quarter Ruler, cut:

• 13 (3⅜"-wide) strips. From strips, cut 138 (3⅜") squares. Cut squares in half diagonally to make 276 half-square B triangles.

• 4 (3"-wide) strips. From strips, cut 48 (3") A squares.

From green batik, cut:

• 9 (3"-wide) strips. From strips, cut 8 (3" × 15½") D rectangles, 4 (3" × 5½") E rectangles, 24 (3") A squares and 52 half-square B triangles.

NOTE: If not using the Fons & Porter Half & Quarter Ruler, cut:

• 3 (3⅜"-wide) strips. From strips, cut 26 (3⅜") squares. Cut squares in half diagonally to make 52 half-square B triangles.

• 6 (3"-wide) strips. From strips, cut 8 (3" × 15½") D rectangles, 4 (3" × 5½") E rectangles, and 24 (3") A squares.

From rust batik, cut:

• 7 (5½"-wide) strips. Piece strips to make 2 (5½" × 65½") top and bottom outer borders and 2 (5½" × 55½") side outer borders.

• 8 (2¼"-wide) strips for binding.

Block Assembly

1. Join 1 tan B triangle and 1 dark B triangle as shown in *Triangle-Square Diagrams*. Make 276 triangle-squares.

Triangle-Square Diagrams

2. Set aside 24 green triangle-squares and 4 green A squares for border.

3. Referring to *Center Unit Diagrams*, place 1 dark A square atop 1 tan C square, right sides facing. Stitch diagonally from corner to corner as shown. Trim ¼" beyond stitching. Press open to reveal triangle. Repeat for remaining corners, using matching dark A squares, to complete 1 Center Unit. Make 13 Center Units.

Center Unit Diagrams

4. Lay out 8 matching triangle-squares, 4 tan A squares, and 2 pairs of matching batik A squares as shown in *Block 1 Assembly Diagram*. Join into rows; join rows to complete 1 Block 1 *(Block 1 Diagram)*. Make 12 Block 1.

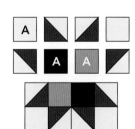

Block 1 Assembly Diagram

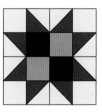

Block 1 Diagram

5. Lay out 1 Center Unit and 12 triangle-squares as shown in *Block 2 Assembly Diagram*. Join into rows; join rows to complete 1 Block 2 *(Block 2 Diagram)*. Make 13 Block 2.

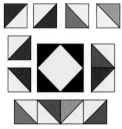

Block 2 Assembly Diagram

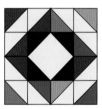

Block 2 Diagram

Border Assembly

1. Referring to *Quilt Top Assembly Diagram* on page 75, join 2 green D rectangles, 6 green triangle-squares, and 2 green A squares as shown to make 1 pieced side inner border. Make 2 pieced side inner borders.

2. Join 2 green D rectangles, 6 green triangle-squares, and 2 green E rectangles to make pieced top inner border. Repeat for pieced bottom inner border.

Quilt Assembly

1. Lay out blocks as shown in *Quilt Top Assembly Diagram*. Join blocks into rows; join rows to complete quilt center.

2. Add pieced side inner borders to quilt center. Add pieced top and bottom inner borders to quilt.

3. Repeat for outer borders.

Finishing

1. Divide backing into 2 (2-yard) lengths. Cut 1 piece in half lengthwise to make 2 narrow panels. Join 1 narrow panel to each side of wider panel; press seam allowances toward narrow panels.

2. Layer backing, batting, and quilt top; baste. Quilt as desired. Quilt shown was outline quilted and has leaf designs in blocks and inner borders *(Quilting Diagram)*.

3. Join 2¼"-wide rust strips into 1 continuous piece for straight-grain French-fold binding. Add binding to quilt.

Quilting Diagram

Quilt Top Assembly Diagram

TRIED & TRUE

Choose sweet pastel colors for a feminine look. Fabrics are from the Juliet's Song collection by Anna Fishkin for Red Rooster Fabrics.

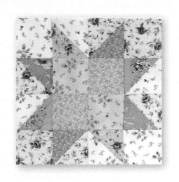

DESIGNER

Bev Getschel fell in love with quilting in 2003, after having sewn all her life. She is the winner of several awards, and is regularly published in quilting magazines.

QUILT BY **June Jaeger.**

Horse Play

Silhouetted stallions give a sense of western adventure to June Jaeger's small quilt. Muted batiks for the center star mimic a hazy high noon sun; sheriffs' badges encircled with dots of white paint anchor each corner of the border.

PROJECT RATING: EASY
Size: 38" × 38"

MATERIALS

4 (8") squares assorted batik prints for center appliqué background
¾ yard tan print batik for background
1 fat quarter★ rust print batik for star points
⅝ yard brown print batik for border
1 fat quarter★ black solid for horse and circle appliqués
9" square gold print for stars
⅜ yard brown stripe for binding
Paper-backed fusible web
White fabric paint (optional)
1¼ yards backing fabric
Crib-size quilt batting
★fat quarter = 18" × 20"

Cutting

Measurements include ¼" seam allowances. Patterns for appliqué pieces are on pages 79–81. Follow manufacturer's instructions for using fusible web.

From tan print batik, cut:
• 1 (8⅜"-wide) strip. From strip, cut 4 (8⅜") squares. Cut squares in half diagonally to make 8 half-square B triangles.
• 1 (8"-wide) strip. From strip, cut 4 (8") A squares.
• 1 (4½"-wide) strip. From strip, cut 4 (4½") border corner squares.

From rust print batik, cut:
• 2 (8⅜"-wide) strips. From strips, cut 4 (8⅜") squares. Cut squares in half diagonally to make 8 half-square B triangles.

From brown print batik, cut:
• 4 (4½"-wide) strips. From strips, cut 4 (4½" × 30½") borders.

From black solid, cut:
- 2 Horses.
- 4 Circles.

From gold print, cut:
- 4 Stars.

From brown stripe, cut:
- 5 (2¼"-wide) strips for binding.

Block Assembly

1. Join the assorted 8" batik squares to form a four-patch as shown in *Center Diagram.*

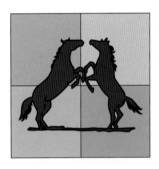

Center Diagram

2. Fuse horses to center four-patch. Straight stitch around appliqué shapes and along dotted detail lines.

3. Join 1 tan print B triangle and 1 rust print B triangle to make a triangle-square. Make 8 triangle-squares.

4. Lay out center, triangle-squares, and tan print A squares as shown in *Quilt Top Assembly Diagram.* Join into sections as shown; join sections to complete quilt center.

5. Add side borders to quilt center.

6. Referring to *Corner Square Diagram,* fuse star atop black circle; straight stitch around star. Fuse black circle to border corner square. If desired, paint white dots around edge of black circle. Straight stitch around edge of circle. Make 4 corner squares.

Quilt Top Assembly Diagram

Corner Square Diagram

7. Add 1 corner square to each end of remaining borders. Add borders to top and bottom of quilt.

Finishing

1. Layer backing, batting, and quilt top; baste. Quilt as desired. Quilt shown has a diagonal grid in the center star and leaf designs in the background and border.

2. Join 2¼"-wide brown stripe strips into 1 continuous piece for straight-grain French-fold binding. Add binding to quilt.

Black iron cutouts were a signature design of Thomas Molesworth's Shoshone Furniture Co. in Cody, Wyoming, in the 1930s. Gene Autry movies created a market for cowboy style, and Molesworth's designs became popular across the country.

Patterns are shown full
size and are reversed for use
with fusible web. Add $^3/_{16}$" seam
allowance for hand appliqué.

TRIED & TRUE

For a tropical look,
substitute palm trees
for the stallions,
and set them on
a background of
bright batik. ✳

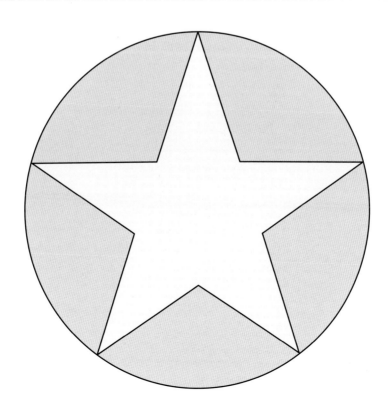

Charming Diamonds

Collecting and swapping fabrics for this multi-fabric quilt is half the fun of making it.
You can make yours as a charm quilt, with no two fabrics repeated for the diamonds as
Shon McMain did, or use multiples of the same fabrics.

PROJECT RATING: CHALLENGING

Size: 52" × 49⅝"

Blocks: 7 diamond cubes

MATERIALS

225 (5") charm squares of assorted
light, medium, and dark batik
fabrics

2½ yards tan batik for background,
borders, and binding

3½ yards fabric for backing

Spray-on fusible web or temporary
adhesive spray designed for use
on fabric

55" × 60" piece of quilt batting

Cutting

Measurements include ¼" seam allowances.

Note: See *Sew Easy: Working with
60-degree Diamonds* on page 86 for tips
on how to cut and join diamonds.

**From each assorted batik fabric
square, cut:**

• 1 (2½"-wide) strip. From strip,
cut 1 (60-degree) diamond.

From tan print, cut:

• 1 (52"-long) piece. From this, cut:

  • 6 (4½"-wide) **lengthwise** border
  strips.

  • 1 (6½"-wide) **lengthwise** strip.
  Using 60-degree angle guide on
  your ruler, cut strip into 6 (6½")
  setting diamonds.

• 1 (12"-wide) strip. From strip, cut
2 (12" × 20") rectangles. With right
sides facing, cut diagonally from corner
to corner, cutting each rectangle into
2 setting triangles for the top and
bottom corners. *(These are oversized
and will be trimmed after they are
attached to quilt.)*

• 6 (2¼"-wide) strips for binding.

Block Assembly

1. Sort diamonds by similar color and
value into 21 sets of 9 diamonds. You
will have 36 diamonds remaining for
the border.

2. Choose 1 set of 9 diamonds. Join 3
diamonds into a row. Make 3 rows.
Join rows to make large diamond.

3. Make 21 large diamonds.

4. Lay out 3 large diamonds to form cube, placing medium value diamond at top of cube, light value diamond on left side, and dark value diamond on right side.

5. Join light diamond and dark diamond, starting and stopping stitching ¼" from ends of seam. This leaves the outer seam allowances free to allow for setting in pieces. Set medium diamond into top edge to complete cube.

6. Make 7 cubes.

Quilt Assembly

1. Referring to *Quilt Top Assembly Diagram*, lay out cubes in 3 rows with 2 cubes in top row, 3 cubes in middle row, and 2 cubes in bottom row. Join cubes into rows; join rows.

2. Make a larger cube by setting 1 tan diamond into opening between cubes in the top and bottom rows and 2 diamonds into openings along each side of quilt.

3. Join tan setting triangles to top left and top right quilt corners and to bottom left and bottom right corners. Use a long ruler and rotary cutter and "square-up" the quilt as needed, leaving ¼" seam allowances beyond corners of patchwork pieces.

4. Measure quilt length. Cut 2 (4½"-wide) border strips to this measurement. Sew borders to quilt sides. Measure quilt width; cut 2 (4½"-wide) border strips to this measurement. Sew borders to top and bottom edges.

5. Measure quilt length; cut 2 (4½"-wide) border strips to this measurement. Sew borders to quilt sides.

6. Arrange 9 diamonds along each outer border. Spray the back of 1 diamond at a time with spray fusible web or temporary adhesive and position on border, keeping in mind ¼" seam allowances. Follow manufacturer's instructions for using spray products.

7. Machine appliqué diamonds to quilt borders. Shon used monofilament nylon thread and a zigzag stitch for her quilt.

Quilting and Finishing

1. Divide backing into 2 (1¾-yard) lengths. Cut 1 piece in half length-wise. Sew 1 narrow panel to 1 side of wider panel. Remaining narrow panel is extra and can be used to make a hanging sleeve.

2. Layer backing, batting, and quilt top; baste. Quilt as desired. Quilt shown was machine quilted in-the-ditch along seams forming cubes. Border diamonds were quilted ¼" from edges. Background was quilted in a meandering flower and leaf design.

3. Join 2¼"-wide tan print strips into 1 continuous piece for straight-grain French-fold binding. Add binding to quilt.

Quilt Top Assembly Diagram

Try This Easy Design Trick

Shon tried out several arrangements of her large, pieced diamonds before she joined them into cubes and assembled the cubes for her quilt top. To help her evaluate her ideas, she took Polaroid™ photos. (Print-outs of digital photos would work equally well.) By looking at the photos side-by-side, she could choose the arrangement she liked best.

Working with 60-degree Diamonds

Single diamonds and groups of diamonds joined into a strip are easy to cut with a rotary cutter and ruler with 60-degree angle markings. Once you've cut the diamonds, follow our easy instructions to join rows of diamonds into larger, pieced diamonds, and then diamond cubes.

Cutting Single Diamonds

1. Begin by cutting a strip of desired width. For the diamonds in *Charming Diamonds* on page 82, cut a 2½"-wide strip. Align the 60-degree angle mark on your ruler with 1 long edge of strip. Cut along edge of ruler, trimming end of strip at a 60-degree angle (*Photo A*).

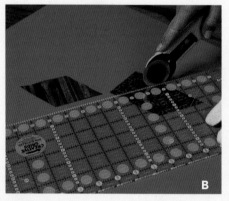

B

C

D

A

2. Turn the trimmed strip and align the 60-degree guide on ruler with 1 long edge of strip and the 2½" strip width guide on ruler with angled cut edge. Cut along ruler to cut 1 diamond (*Photo B*).

Making Large, Pieced Diamonds

1. For the *Charming Diamonds* quilt on page 82, small diamonds are arranged in 3 rows of 3 diamonds in the large, pieced diamonds. Begin by cutting 1 (2½"-wide) strip each of 9 different fabrics for the small diamonds. Join strips into 3 strip sets with 3 strips in each strip set, off-setting strips at 1 end by approximately 1½" (*Photo C*). Press seam allowances to 1 side.

2. Align 60-degree angle cutting guide on ruler with 1 long edge of 1 strip set. Cut along edge of ruler (*Photo D*).

3. Align 60-degree guide on ruler with one long edge of 1 strip set and 2½"

strip width guide on ruler with angled cut edge. Cut along ruler to cut 1 (3-diamond) row (*Photo E*). Cut desired number of 3-diamond rows from strip set. Repeat to cut 3-diamond rows from other 2 strip sets.

E

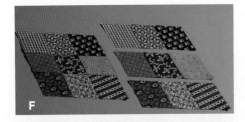

F

G

H

4. Lay out 3-diamond rows as shown in *Photo F*. Join rows to make large diamond, matching diamond seams ¼" from raw edge as shown in *Photo G*.

5. If diamonds do not match, give them the "pinch test" by pinching a slightly deeper seam with your fingers. If the alignment becomes worse (*Photo H*), your seam was too wide. You will need to pick out the the seam where diamonds meet and restitch with a slightly narrower seam. If the alignment improves with pinching, restitch with a slightly wider seam at diamond intersections.

Making a Cube

1. To prepare to make a cube as shown in *Photo I*, choose fabrics for 2 more large diamonds. Cut strips, join into strip sets, and cut 3-diamond rows as directed in steps #1– #3 on previous page. Join 3-diamond rows into large diamond. Make 2 large diamonds.

2. Pin left and right diamonds together, aligning small diamond seams. To secure seam without stitching in reverse, position large diamonds "backwards" in sewing machine (*Photo J*). Sew forward to the beginning point of seam (¼" from raw edge) and pivot with needle down.

3. Sew forward, taking ¼" seam (*Photo K*). Stop stitching ¼" from end of diamonds, pivot so work is again "backwards" in the sewing machine, and sew forward a few stitches to secure end of seam. The seam allowances at the beginning and end of the seam should be free to allow for setting in pieces.

4. Set top large diamond into opening between left and right large diamonds. Pin top diamond to 1 side diamond. Stitch seam, starting and stopping stitching ¼" from ends of seams as before to allow for setting in pieces (*Photo L*).

5. Pin top large diamond to the other side diamond, matching small diamond seams (*Photo M*). Join diamonds to complete cube (*Photo N*), leaving ends of seams free.

J

K

L

M

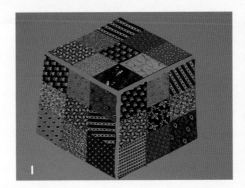

I

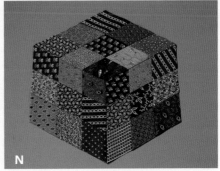

N

Sailing

Batiks are perfect for this dramatic wallhanging by Lori Hein. The borders add dimension to this golden sunset on a deep blue background.

MATERIALS

¼ yard dark orange/green batik for borders #1 and #6

⅝ yard dark green batik for borders #2 and #6

¼ yard light orange/green batik for sand dollars and border #3

1 yard blue batik for water and borders #4 and #6

⅞ yard yellow stripe batik for sky and border #5

5 fat quarters★★ assorted green, purple, and blue batiks for border #6

3" square bright orange batik for sun

1 fat eighth★ light orange batik for starfish

5" × 9" rectangle black solid for sailboat

½ yard dark blue batik for binding

Paper-backed fusible web

Black and light orange embroidery floss

3 yards backing fabric

Twin-size quilt batting

★fat eighth = 9" × 20"

★★fat quarter = 18" × 20"

PROJECT RATING: EASY

Size: 48" × 52"

Cutting

Measurements include ¼" seam allowances. Border strips are exact length needed. You may want to make them longer to allow for piecing variations. Patterns for appliqué are on page 91. Follow manufacturer's instructions for using fusible web.

From dark orange/green batik, cut:

- 1 (2½"-wide) strip. Cut strip in half to make 2 (2½" × 20") strips for strip sets.
- 2 (1½"-wide) strips. From strips, cut 2 (1½" × 21") side border #1 and 2 (1½" × 19") top and bottom border #1.

From dark green batik, cut:

- 4 (3"-wide) strips. From strips, cut 2 (3" × 24") top and bottom border #2 and 2 (3" × 23") side border #2.

- 2 (2½"-wide) strips. Cut strips in half to make 4 (2½" × 20") strips for strip sets.

From light orange/green batik, cut:

- 4 (1½"-wide) strips. From strips, cut 2 (1½" × 28") side border #3 and 2 (1½" × 26") top and bottom border #3.
- 4 Large Sand Dollars.
- 4 Medium Sand Dollars.
- 4 Small Sand Dollars.

From blue batik, cut:

- 1 (10¾"-wide) strip. From strip, cut 1 (10¾" × 17") rectangle.
- 4 (4¼"-wide) strips. From strips, cut 2 (4¼" × 33½") top and bottom border #4 and 2 (4¼" × 30") side border #4.
- 2 (2½"-wide) strips. Cut strips in half to make 4 (2½" × 20") strips for strip sets.

From yellow stripe batik, cut:

- 1 (17"-wide) strip. From strip, cut 1 (17" × 10¾") rectangle.
- 4 (2"-wide) strips. From strips, cut 2 (2" × 37½") side border #5 and 2 (2" × 36½") top and bottom border #5.

From each fat quarter, cut:

- 6 (2½"-wide) strips for strip sets.

From bright orange batik, cut:
• 1 Sun (Use Large Sand Dollar Circle pattern).

From light orange batik, cut:
• 8 Starfish.

From black solid, cut:
• 1 Large Sail.
• 1 Small Sail.
• 1 Boat.

From dark blue batik, cut:
• 6 (2¼"-wide) strips for binding.

Outer Border Assembly

1. Join 3 (2½"-wide) assorted batik strips as shown in *Strip Set Diagram*. Make 13 strip sets. From strip sets, cut 88 (2½"-wide) segments.

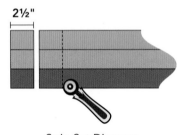

2½"

Strip Set Diagram

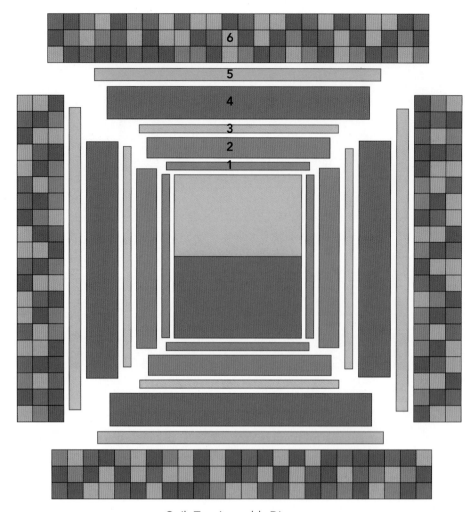

Quilt Top Assembly Diagram

2. Join 20 segments to make 1 side border #6 as shown in *Quilt Top Assembly Diagram*. Make 2 side border #6.

3. In the same manner, join 24 segments to make top border #6. Repeat for bottom border #6.

Quilt Assembly

1. Join blue batik rectangle and yellow stripe batik rectangle to make quilt center as shown in *Quilt Top Assembly Diagram*.

2. Referring to photo on page 88 for placement, fuse sun, small sail, large sail, and boat on quilt center. Machine appliqué pieces using matching thread and a narrow zigzag stitch.

3. Add dark orange/green batik side border #1 to quilt center. Add top and bottom border #1 to quilt.

4. Add borders #2–#6 in the same manner.

5. Referring to photo for placement, fuse starfish and sand dollars on quilt. Machine appliqué sand dollars using matching thread and narrow zigzag stitch. Hand appliqué starfish using light orange embroidery floss and blanket stitch.

6. Embroider details on sand dollars using black embroidery floss.

Finishing

1. Divide backing into 2 (1½-yard) lengths. Cut 1 piece in half lengthwise to make 2 narrow panels. Join 1 narrow panel to wider panel. Remaining panel is extra and can be used to make a hanging sleeve.

2. Layer backing, batting, and quilt top; baste. Quilt as desired. Quilt shown was quilted with horizontal lines in the sky, meandering in the water, and with waves, sand dollars, starfish, and seashells in the borders *(Quilting Diagram on page 91)*.

3. Join 2¼"-wide dark blue batik strips into 1 continuous piece for straight-grain French-fold binding. Add binding to quilt.

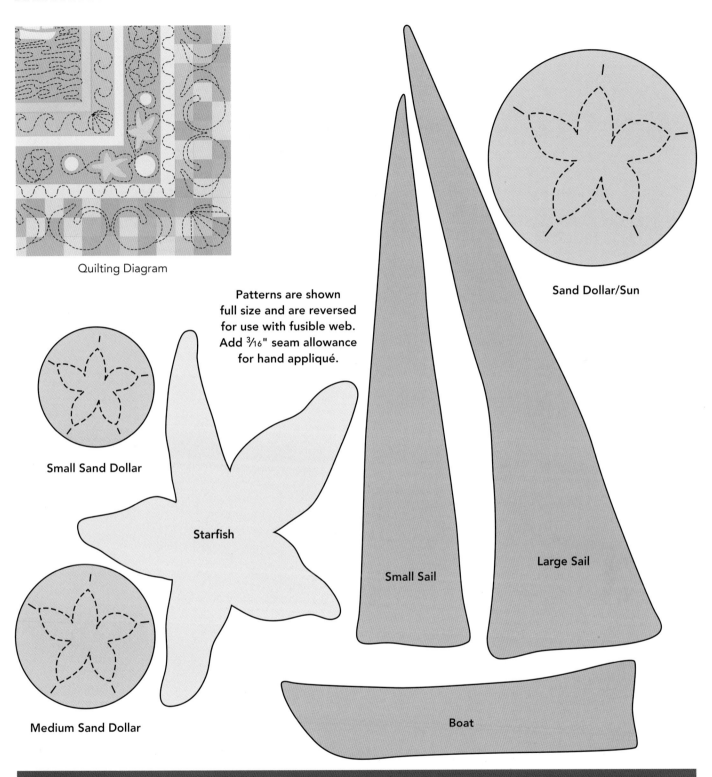

Quilting Diagram

Patterns are shown
full size and are reversed
for use with fusible web.
Add ³⁄₁₆" seam allowance
for hand appliqué.

Sand Dollar/Sun

Small Sand Dollar

Starfish

Small Sail

Large Sail

Medium Sand Dollar

Boat

DESIGNER

Lori Hein was introduced to quilting in 1983, when she was a young mother of three, living on her husband's family homestead near Spokane, Washington. She immediately loved working with the fabrics and block designs. When her children were nearly raised, Lori began working at a quilt shop, teaching classes, and designing her own quilt patterns. In 2005, she launched her on line company, Cool Water Quilts. ✳

Sunflowers

Inspired by the bright sunflowers in the border batik, artist and author Shelly Stokes designed this gorgeous wall quilt using her Paintstiks® stencil technique.

PROJECT RATING: INTERMEDIATE

Size: 34½" × 34½"

MATERIALS

1 fat quarter★ each bright red, green, blue, pink, and orange batik for blocks

¾ yard sunflower print batik for outer border

¼ yard yellow batik for accent strips

½ yard purple batik for inner border and binding

1⅛ yards backing fabric

Freezer paper

Craft knife

Masking tape

½"-diameter stencil brush

Shiva® Artist's Paintstiks® in Prussian Blue, Sap Green, and Alizarin Crimson.

Crib-size quilt batting

★fat quarter = 18" × 20"

Cutting

Pattern for Sunflower template is on page 97. Measurements include ¼" seam allowances. Border strips are exact length needed. You may want to make them longer to allow for piecing variations.

From each fat quarter, cut:

• 1 (12") square.

From sunflower print batik, cut:

• 4 (6"-wide) strips. From strips, cut 2 (6" × 24") side outer borders, and 2 (6" × 35") top and bottom outer borders.

From yellow batik, cut:

• 4 (⅞"-wide) strips. From strips, cut 4 (⅞" × 22½") accent strips and 4 (⅞" × 11½") accent strips.

From purple batik, cut:

• 4 (1¼"-wide) strips. From strips, cut 2 (1¼" × 22½") side inner borders and 2 (1¼" × 24") top and bottom inner borders.

• 4 (2¼"-wide) strips for binding.

Block Assembly

1. Following instructions in *Sew Easy: Using Paintstiks® on Fabric* on pages 96–97, stencil a sunflower on each 12" batik square. Allow to dry; heat set.

2. Cut each 12" batik square in half in both directions to make 4 (6") squares. (You will have a few extra.)

Quilt Assembly

1. Lay out 4 center squares as shown in *Quilt Top Assembly Diagram* on page 94. Join squares to complete center unit.

2. Fold 1 (11½"-long) yellow accent strip in half lengthwise, wrong sides together; press.

3. Align raw edges of folded accent strip with side of center square; baste in place. Repeat for remaining three sides.

4. Referring to *Quilt Top Assembly Diagram*, lay out remaining squares. Join squares and center unit into rows; join rows to complete quilt center.

5. Fold 1 (22½"-long) yellow accent strip in half lengthwise, wrong sides together; press. Align raw edges of folded accent strip with side of quilt center; baste in place. Repeat for remaining three sides.

6. Add purple side inner borders to quilt center. Add top and bottom inner borders to quilt. Repeat for outer borders.

Finishing

1. Layer backing, batting, and quilt top; baste. Quilt as desired. Quilt shown was quilted around the sunflowers in the center and border and has a swirled freehand design in the center background *(Quilting Diagram)*.

2. Join 2¼"-wide purple batik strips into 1 continuous piece for straight-grain French-fold binding. Add binding to quilt.

Quilt Top Assembly Diagram

DESIGNER

Shelly Stokes, award winning quilter and author of *Paintstiks on Fabric*, started quilting in 1995, after leaving the corporate world. Eventually, she began experimenting with dyes and exploring the world of fiber art. She founded Cedar Canyon Textiles in 1997 to sell her hand-dyed fabric and artwork. ✳

Quilting Diagram

Rubbing Plates make it easy to create interesting Paintstik textures on fabric. Aside from the standard bird and flower plates you can find, among others, motifs inspired by Asian, Greek, African, and Ukranian cultures, and even groovy geometric patterns. You can also create textures by using household items such as keys, place mats, coins, and doilies.

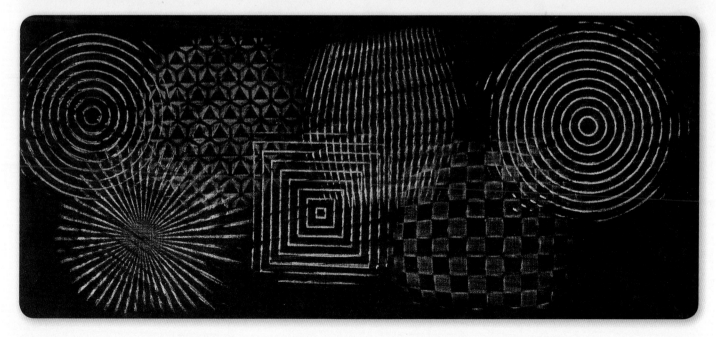

Sew Easy™

Using Paintstiks® on Fabric

BY **Shelly Stokes**.

Painting on fabric with Shiva® Artist's Paintstiks is a simple way to embellish your favorite hand-dyed or commercial fabric.

A

B

C

D

Making A Stencil

1. Cut a 12" square of freezer paper; fold paper in half and in half again to make a 6" square.

2. Using the Sunflower pattern on page 97, trace the stencil design onto the folded freezer paper (*Photo A*).

3. Place folded paper on cutting mat and use a craft knife to cut through all layers of paper (*Photo B*). Unfold paper to reveal complete stencil.

Painting

1. Prewash fabric using plain detergent. **Do not use fabric softener.** Iron freezer paper stencil to right side of fabric. Tape fabric to work surface.

2. Before painting, remove protective skin from Paintstik. "Pinch" skin off with a paper towel or carefully peel it away with a small, sharp knife.

3. Apply color to a paper palette (parchment paper or several strips of masking tape on paper work well). Load paint onto stencil brush.

4. Hold stencil brush at a 90-degree angle and, using a gentle, circular motion, apply paint to fabric surface (*Photo C*). Use a different color of paint in each quarter of the stencil to create varied effects. Carefully remove stencil from fabric (*Photo D*).

Adding Texture with Rubbings

1. Attach prewashed fabric to work surface, right side up, using masking tape on three sides.

2. Slide the textured surface between the fabric and work surface, making sure fabric remains taut.

3. Rub the Paintstik on a paper towel until the end has a smooth, flat surface.

4. Apply the Paintstik directly to the fabric over the textured surface, using even strokes, moving in one direction only *(Photo E)*.

5. Move the textured surface to a new location under your fabric and make an additional rubbing.

Setting Paint

1. Allow paint to dry on fabric 2–3 days before heat setting.

2. To heat set design, place fabric **paint side down** on grease-proof paper (such as parchment paper) to protect ironing surface. Press each section of fabric for 10–15 seconds. Use the highest temperature setting appropriate for your fabric.

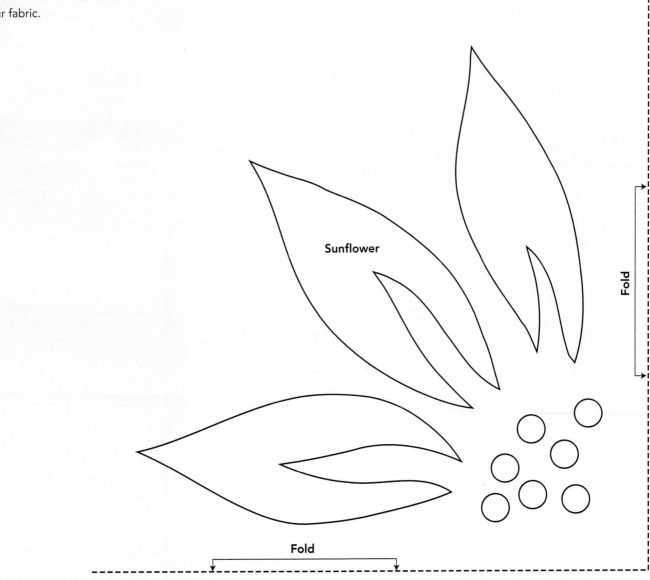

Sunflower

Fold

Fold

Night Blooms

Designer Nancy Mahoney created red-orange hothouse blossoms that stand out against a background of cool blues.

PROJECT RATING: INTERMEDIATE

Size: 62" × 80"

Blocks: 18 (9") Nine Patch blocks
17 (9") Flower blocks

MATERIALS

2¼ yards light blue print for blocks

1¾ yard medium blue print for inner and outer borders

¼ yard green print for middle border

7 fat quarters★ assorted medium/dark blue prints for blocks

3 fat quarters★ assorted orange prints for flowers

2 fat quarters★ assorted green prints for leaves

1 fat quarter★ gold print for large flower centers

1 fat quarter★ dark orange print for small flower centers

⅝ yard dark blue print for binding

Paper-backed fusible web

5 yards backing fabric

Full-size quilt batting

★fat quarter = 18" × 20"

Cutting

Measurements include ¼" seam allowances. Border strips are exact length needed. You may want to make them longer to allow for piecing variations. Patterns for appliqué shapes are on page 102. Follow manufacturer's instructions for using fusible web.

From light blue print, cut:

- 5 (9½"-wide) strips. From strips, cut 17 (9½") A squares.
- 7 (3½"-wide) strips. From strips, cut 72 (3½") B squares.

From medium blue print, cut:

- 7 (6¾"-wide) strips. Piece strips to make 2 (6¾" × 68") side outer borders and 2 (6¾" × 62½") top and bottom outer borders.
- 6 (2"-wide) strips. Piece strips to make 2 (2" × 63½") side inner borders and 2 (2" × 48½") top and bottom inner borders.

From green print, cut:

- 6 (1¼"-wide) strips. Piece strips to make 2 (1¼" × 66½") side middle borders and 2 (1¼" × 50") top and bottom middle borders.

From each medium/dark blue print fat quarter, cut:

• 5 (3½"-wide) strips. From strips, cut 23 (3½") B squares.

From each orange print fat quarter, cut:

• 6 Flowers.

From each green print fat quarter, cut:

• 34 Leaves.

From gold print fat quarter, cut:

• 17 Large Centers.

From dark orange print fat quarter, cut:

• 17 Small Centers.

From dark blue print, cut:

• 8 (2¼"-wide) strips for binding.

Nine Patch Block Assembly

1. Lay out 5 medium/dark blue B squares and 4 light blue B squares as shown in *Nine Patch Block Assembly Diagram*.

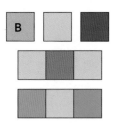

Nine Patch Block Assembly Diagram

2. Join into horizontal rows; join rows to complete 1 Nine Patch block *(Nine Patch Block Diagram)*. Make 18 Nine Patch blocks.

Nine Patch Block Diagram

Flower Block Assembly

1. Choose 4 medium/dark blue B squares. Referring to *Background Assembly Diagrams*, place 1 B square atop 1 light blue A square, right sides facing. Stitch diagonally from corner to corner as shown. Trim ¼" beyond stitching. Press open to reveal triangle. Repeat for 3 remaining corners to complete 1 Flower block background.

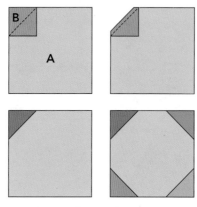

Background Assembly Diagrams

2. Referring to *Flower Block Diagram*, fuse 1 Flower, 1 Large Center, 1 Small Center, and 4 Leaves on block background. Machine blanket stitch around pieces using matching thread. Make 17 Flower blocks.

Flower Block Diagram

Quilt Assembly

1. Lay out Nine Patch and Flower blocks as shown in *Quilt Top Assembly Diagram* on page 101.

2. Join into rows; join rows to complete quilt center.

3. Add medium blue print side inner borders to quilt center. Add top and bottom inner borders to quilt. Repeat for green print middle borders and medium blue print outer borders.

Finishing

1. Divide backing into 2 (2½-yard) lengths. Cut 1 piece in half lengthwise to make 2 narrow panels. Join 1 narrow panel to each side of wider panel; press seam allowances toward narrow panels.

2. Layer backing, batting, and quilt top; baste. Quilt as desired. Quilt shown was outline quilted around the appliqués, quilted in the ditch between blocks and borders, and has freehand designs in the blocks and borders *(Quilting Diagram)*.

3. Join 2¼"-wide dark blue strips into 1 continuous piece for straight-grain French-fold binding. Add binding to quilt.

Quilting Diagram

Quilt Top Assembly Diagram

WEB EXTRA

Go to www.FonsandPorter.com/bloomssizes
to download *Quilt Top Assembly Diagrams* for
these size options. ✳

SIZE OPTIONS

	Wallhanging (36" × 36")	Full (80" × 80")	Queen (98" × 98")
Blocks	5 Nine Patch blocks	25 Nine Patch blocks	41 Nine Patch blocks
	4 Flower blocks	24 Flower blocks	40 Flower blocks
Setting	3 × 3 blocks	7 × 7 blocks	9 × 9 blocks

MATERIALS

	Wallhanging (36" × 36")	Full (80" × 80")	Queen (98" × 98")
Light blue print	¾ yard	2¾ yards	4¼ yards
Medium blue print	1¼ yards	2 yards	2½ yards
Green print for middle border	¼ yard	½ yard	⅝ yard
Medium/dark blue prints	2 fat quarters	11 fat quarters	19 fat quarters
Orange prints	1 fat quarter	4 fat quarters	7 fat quarters
Green prints	1 fat eighth or scraps	3 fat quarters	4 fat quarters
Gold print	scraps	1 fat quarter	2 fat quarters
Dark orange print	scraps	1 fat eighth	1 fat quarter
Binding	⅜ yard	¾ yard	⅞ yard
Backing Fabric	1¼ yards	8¼ yards	9 yards
Batting	Crib-size	Queen-size	King-size

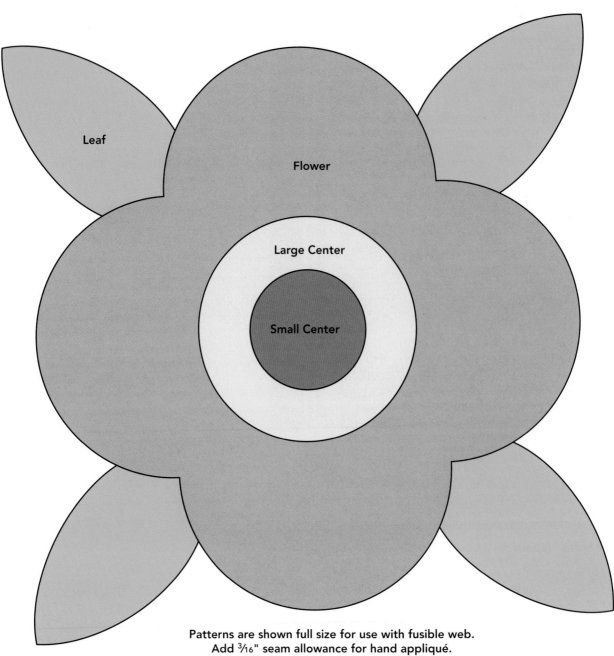

Leaf

Flower

Large Center

Small Center

**Patterns are shown full size for use with fusible web.
Add ³⁄₁₆" seam allowance for hand appliqué.**

TRIED & TRUE

Nancy Mahoney made a wallhanging using reproduction
1930s prints to create a soft, old-fashioned look. Yardage
requirements are given in the chart on page 101. ✳

DESIGNER

A prolific quiltmaker, Nancy Mahoney is also an author, teacher, and fabric designer. She enjoys making traditional quilts using new techniques that make quiltmaking easier and fun.

Gold Rush

Designer Joanne Fiorino uses a simple Double Four Patch block in two color variations for this quilt. By turning the blocks different ways, Joanne creates chains of small squares running diagonally across the quilt top.

PROJECT RATING: EASY

Finished Size: 49" × 49"

Blocks: 36 (7") Double Four Patch blocks (18 light and 18 dark)

MATERIALS

6 fat quarters★ assorted light batiks for blocks and borders

9 fat quarters★ assorted dark batiks for blocks and borders

½ yard light batik for binding

3¼ yards backing fabric

Twin-size quilt batting

★fat quarter = 18" × 20"

Cutting

Measurements include ¼" seam allowances.

From each light batik fat quarter, cut:

• 3 (2¼"-wide) strips for strip sets.

• 2 (4"-wide) strips. From strips, cut 6 (4") A squares.

• 1 (2¼"-wide) strip. From strip, cut 4 (2¼") D squares.

From each dark batik fat quarter, cut:

• 2 (2¼"-wide) strips for strip sets.

• 1 (4"-wide) strip. From strip, cut 4 (4") A squares.

From remaining pieces of dark batik fat quarters, cut:

• 4 (4" × 14½") B border rectangles.

• 8 (4" × 11") C border rectangles.

• 2 (4") A squares for border corners.

• 20 (2¼") D squares for border units.

From light batik, cut:

• 6 (2¼"-wide) strips for binding.

Block Assembly

1. Join 1 light (2¼"-wide) strip and 1 dark (2¼"-wide) strip as shown in *Strip Set Diagram*. From strip set, cut 8 (2¼"-wide) segments.

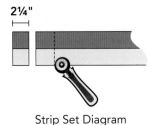

Strip Set Diagram

2. Referring to *Block Assembly Diagram*, join 2 strip set segments to make 1 four patch unit. Make 4 four patch units.

Block Assembly Diagram

3. Lay out 2 four patch units and 2 matching light A squares as shown in *Block Assembly Diagram*. Join into rows; join rows to complete 1 light block *(Light Block Diagram)*. Make 18 light blocks.

Light Block Diagram

4. In the same manner, lay out 2 four patch units and 2 matching dark A squares. Join to complete 1 dark block *(Dark Block Diagram)*. Make 18 dark blocks.

Dark Block Diagram

Border Unit Assembly

1. Choose 2 matching light D squares and 2 matching dark D squares. Join as shown in *Border Unit Diagrams* to complete 1 border unit.

2. Make 10 border units.

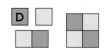

Border Unit Diagrams

Quilt Assembly

1. Lay out light and dark blocks, border units, border rectangles, and border corner squares as shown in *Quilt Top Assembly Diagram*. Join blocks into rows. Join rows to complete quilt center.

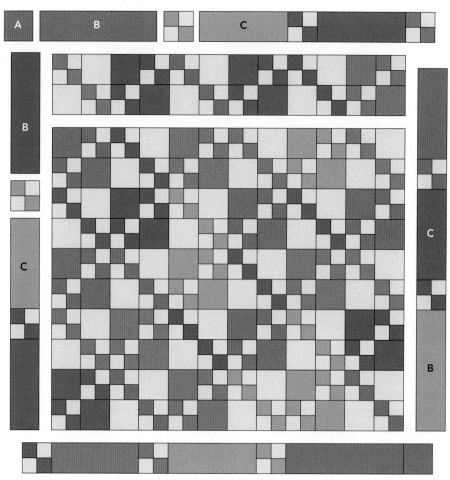

Quilt Top Assembly Diagram

2. Join 1 B rectangle, 2 C rectangles, and 2 border units to make 1 side border. Attach to side of quilt center. Repeat for other side.

3. Join 1 A square, 1 B rectangle, 2 C rectangles, and 3 border units to make top border. Add to top of quilt center. Repeat for bottom.

Finishing

1. Divide backing into 2 (1⅝-yard) pieces. Cut 1 piece in half lengthwise. Join 1 narrow panel to wider panel. Press seam allowances toward narrow panel. Remaining piece is extra and can be used to make a hanging sleeve.

2. Layer backing, batting, and quilt top; baste. Quilt as desired. Quilt shown was quilted with diagonal lines through the chains of small squares.

3. Join 2¼"-wide light batik strips into 1 continuous piece for straight-grain French-fold binding. Add binding to quilt.

SIZE OPTIONS

	Twin (77" × 91")	Queen (91" × 105")
Blocks	60 light & 60 dark	84 light & 84 dark
Setting	10 × 12 blocks	12 × 14 blocks

MATERIALS

Light	20 fat quarters	28 fat quarters
Dark	30 fat quarters	42 fat quarters
Binding	¾ yard	¾ yard
Backing Fabric	5½ yards	8¼ yards
Batting	Full-size	King-size

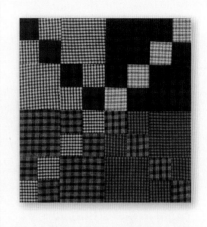

TRIED & TRUE

This plaid group of blocks is made from Moda's Seeds of Time collection by Kansas Troubles. ❋

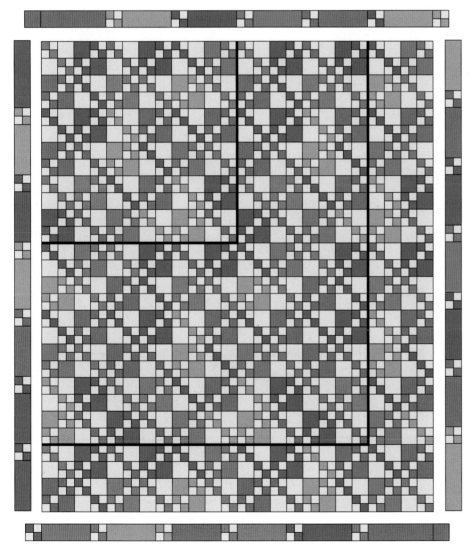

Quilt Top Diagram

(Multiple Sizes Shown)

WALLHANGING	49" x 49"
TWIN	77" x 91"
QUEEN	91" x 105"

Baby Blue Mini

Nancy T. Rogers entered our "Make a Mini" contest.

Her little quilt, inspired by *Gold Rush*, was one of our favorite entries.

PROJECT RATING: EASY

Size: 16" × 16"

Blocks: 40 (2") Double 4 Patch blocks
(20 light and 20 dark)

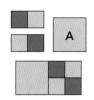

Block Assembly Diagram

Light Block Diagram

Dark Block Diagram

MATERIALS

5 fat eighths★ assorted light blue,
pink, and purple batiks for blocks

5 fat eighths★ assorted dark blue,
pink, and purple batiks for blocks

1 fat quarter★★ medium blue batik
for border

¼ yard dark blue batik for binding

20" square backing fabric

20" square quilt batting

★fat eighth = 9" × 20"

★★fat quarter = 18" × 20"

Cutting

Measurements include ¼" seam
allowances.

From each fat eighth, cut:

• 2 (1"-wide) strips for strip sets.

• 1 (1½"-wide) strip. From strip,
cut 8 (1½") A squares.

From medium blue batik, cut:

• 4 (2½"-wide) strips. From strips,
cut 4 (2½" × 12½") borders.

From dark blue batik, cut:

• 2 (2¼"-wide) strips for binding.

Block Assembly

1. Join 1 light (1"-wide) strip and 1
dark (1"-wide) strip to make a strip as
shown in *Strip Set Diagram*. Make 10
strip sets. From each strip set, cut 16
(1"-wide) segments.

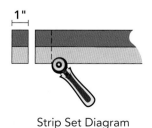

Strip Set Diagram

2. Referring to *Block Assembly Diagram*,
join 2 matching strip set segments to
make a four patch unit. Make 2 four
patch units.

3. Lay out 2 four patch units and 2
matching light A squares as shown
in *Block Assembly Diagram*. Join into
rows; join rows to complete 1 light
block *(Light Block Diagram)*. Make
20 light blocks.

4. In the same manner, lay out 2 four
patch units and 2 matching dark
A squares. Join to complete 1 dark
block *(Dark Block Diagram)*. Make
20 dark blocks.

Quilt Assembly

1. Lay out 18 light and 18 dark blocks,
alternating as shown in *Quilt Top*

Assembly Diagram. Join blocks into
rows; join rows to complete quilt
center.

2. Add side borders to quilt center.

3. Add 1 light block and 1 dark block
to ends of each remaining border
strip. Add borders to top and bottom
of quilt.

Finishing

1. Layer backing, batting, and quilt top;
baste. Quilt as desired. Quilt shown
was quilted with diagonal wavy lines
through the chains of small squares
and into the border.

2. Join 2¼"-wide dark blue strips into
1 continuous piece for straight-grain
French-fold binding. Add binding to
quilt.

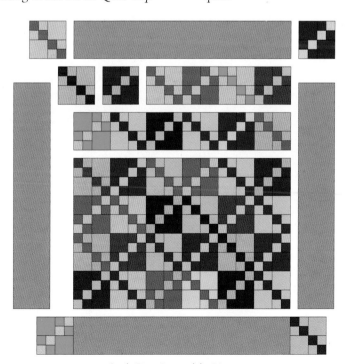

Quilt Top Assembly Diagram

TABLE RUNNER DESIGNED BY **Jodie Davis**.

MADE BY **Jayne Davis**.

Candy Flowers
Table Runner

Colorful buttons adorn fused flowers on this cute table runner.

Size: 14½" × 38½"

MATERIALS

½ yard blue batik for background

⅜ yard light green batik for stems, leaves, and binding

1 fat eighth★ medium green batik

4" × 8" rectangle each red, pink, and orange batiks

5" square turquoise batik

2½" × 5" rectangle purple batik

Paper-backed fusible web

½ yard backing fabric

2 (1⅛"-diameter) yellow buttons

2 (⅞"-diameter) mother of pearl buttons

14 (¾"-diameter) mother of pearl buttons

2 (½"-diameter) mother of pearl buttons

14 (⁷⁄₁₆"-diameter) red buttons

2 (⅝"-diameter) orange buttons

30 (¼"-diameter) orange buttons

14 (¼"-diameter) green buttons

14 (¼"-diameter) yellow buttons

2 (¼"-diameter) purple buttons

18" × 40" rectangle batting

★fat eighth = 9" × 20"

Cutting

Measurements include ¼" seam allowances. Patterns for appliqué shapes are on pages 112 and 113. Follow manufacturer's instructions for using fusible web.

From blue batik, cut:

• 1 (14½"-wide) strip. From strip, cut 1 (14½" × 38½") rectangle.

From light green batik, cut:

• 3 (2¼"-wide) strips for binding.

• 4 A.

• 2 B.

• 6 C.

• 6 D.

• 4 D reversed.

• 4 E.

From medium green batik fat eighth, cut:

• 2 each F, G, H, and I.

• 4 J.

From orange batik, cut:

• 2 K.

From pink batik, cut:

• 2 L.

From red batik, cut:

• 2 M.

From purple batik, cut:

• 2 N.

From turquoise batik, cut:

• 2 O.

Appliqué

1. Referring to table runner photo, arrange appliqué pieces atop blue background rectangle. Fuse in place.

2. Topstitch each piece ¹⁄₁₆" inside edges using matching thread.

Finishing

1. Layer backing, batting, and quilt top; baste. Quilt as desired. Table runner shown was outline quilted ⅛" outside flowers and leaves and with parallel lines 1" apart in center (*Quilting Diagram* on page 112).

2. Join 2¼"-wide light green batik strips into 1 continuous piece for straight-grain French-fold binding. Add binding to quilt.

3. Referring to photo, sew 7 (⁷⁄₁₆") red buttons and 7 (¼") green buttons to each pink flower.

4. Sew 1 (1⅛") yellow button, 1 (⅝") orange button, and 1 (¼") purple button to each orange flower.

5. Sew 15 (¼") orange buttons to each turquoise flower.

6. Sew 1 (⅞") mother of pearl button and 1 (½") mother of pearl button to each red/purple flower.

7. Sew 7 (¾") mother of pearl buttons and 7 (¼") yellow buttons to each stem F.

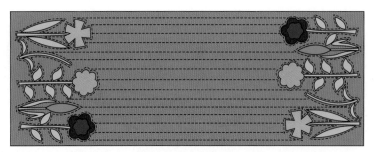

Quilting Diagram

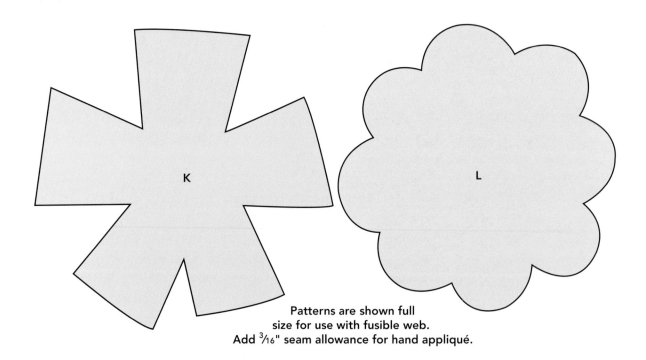

K

L

Patterns are shown full
size for use with fusible web.
Add $^3/_{16}$" seam allowance for hand appliqué.

DESIGNER

Jodie Davis has a busy schedule as host of "Quilt Out Loud" and "Quilt It! The Longarm Quilting Show" on QNNtv.com. She likes to make quilts that are easy and quick so she can share them with her viewers. ✳

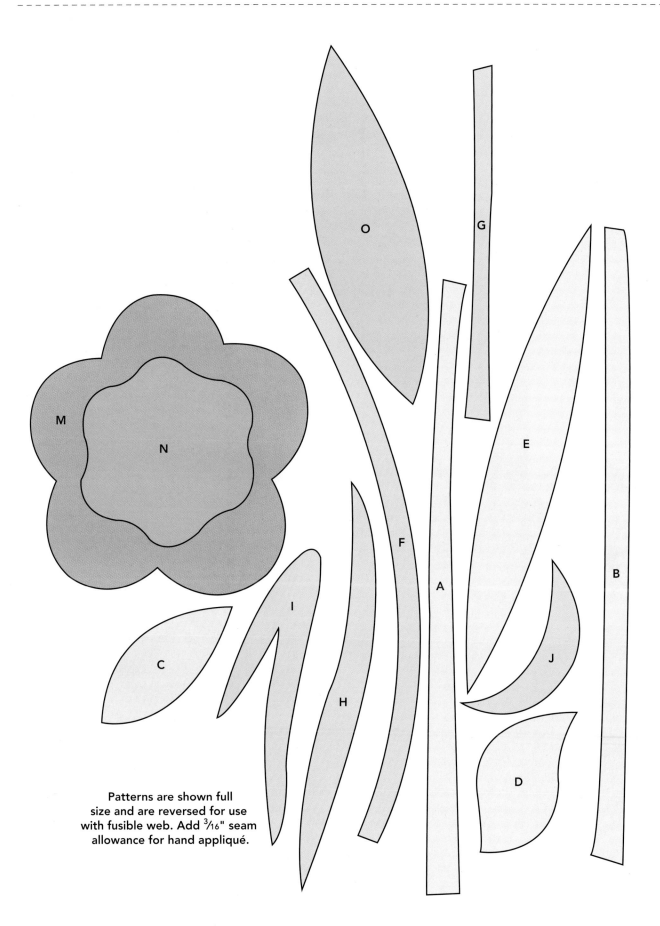

Patterns are shown full
size and are reversed for use
with fusible web. Add $^3/_{16}$" seam
allowance for hand appliqué.

Graceful Ladies

Quilt artist Janet Pittman combines machine appliqué and bobbin work to create clematis blossoms just as beautiful as those she grows in her garden.

PROJECT RATING: INTERMEDIATE
Size: 17" × 25"

MATERIALS

- ¾ yard dark blue batik for background and binding
- 1 fat eighth★ bright orange batik for flower
- 1 fat eighth★ orange stripe batik for inner border
- 1 fat eighth★ bright green solid batik for leaves and stems
- ¼ yard medium blue batik for outer border
- ¾ yard backing fabric
- 20" × 30" quilt batting
- Paper-backed fusible web
- Gold thread for flower centers
- 1 spool cream size 8 pearl cotton

★fat eighth = 9" × 20"

Cutting

Patterns for appliqué shapes are on page 117. Follow manufacturer's instructions for using fusible web. Measurements include ¼" seam allowances. Border strips are exact length needed. You may want to make them longer to allow for piecing variations.

From dark blue batik, cut:
- 1 (12" × 20") rectangle for background.
- 3 (2¼"-wide) strips for binding.

From bright orange batik, cut:
- 12 Flower Petals.

Sew **Smart**™

If orange flower fabric has a linear pattern, cut appliqué so the lines are lengthwise on each petal for a realistic look. —Janet

From orange stripe batik, cut:

- 4 (1"-wide) strips. From strips, cut 2 (1" × 19½") side inner borders and 2 (1" × 12½") top and bottom inner borders.

From bright green batik, cut:

- 1 (10") square for stems. Referring to *Bias Stem Diagrams*, cut square in half diagonally. Place a (1" × 12") piece of fusible web on wrong side of triangle along bias edge. Cut 2 stem strips tapering from ¼"-wide to ⅛"-wide and 1 stem strip ⅛"-wide.
- 8 Leaves.

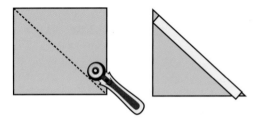

Bias Stem Diagrams

From medium blue batik, cut:

- 2 (3"-wide) strips. From strips, cut: 2 (3" × 20½") side outer borders and 2 (3" × 17½") top and bottom outer borders.

Quilt Center

1. Referring to *Quilt Top Assembly Diagram*, arrange flower petals, leaves, and stems on background. Fuse in place.
2. Referring to *Sew Easy: Bobbin Work* on page 118, embellish the flower petals, leaves, and stems.
3. Using a free-motion foot, stitch the flower centers from the right side with gold thread. Starting near the center of the flower, stitch slightly arcing lines out and back along the same

line. Stitch 15 to 20 arcs. Stitch several overlapping circles in the center.

4. Trim background to 11½" × 19½".

Quilt Assembly

1. Add orange stripe side inner borders to quilt center. Add top and bottom inner borders to quilt.
2. Repeat for blue outer borders.

Quilt Top Assembly Diagram

Finishing

1. Layer backing, batting, and quilt top; baste. Quilt as desired. Quilt shown was outline quilted with invisible thread around the appliqué and with continuous heart-shaped leaves in the background and border.
2. Join 2¼"-wide dark blue strips into 1 continuous piece for straight-grain French-fold binding. Add binding to quilt.

Patterns are shown full
size and are reversed for use
with fusible web. Add $\frac{3}{16}$" seam
allowance for hand appliqué.

Cut 2

Cut 2

Bobbin Work

Try Janet Pittman's technique to embellish appliqué
using pearl cotton in your machine's bobbin.

1. Arrange and fuse appliqué pieces to
   background.
2. Straight stitch a scant ⅛" inside edges
   of appliqué shapes, such as flowers
   and leaves, using matching thread
   in top spool and bobbin (*Photo A*).
   Straight stitch down middle of appliqué stems. Bobbin thread must be a
   color that will show up on wrong side
   of background (*Photo B*).

A

B

3. Wind bobbin with size 8 pearl cotton.
   Loosen tension on bobbin case. (Make
   note of initial position of screwdriver
   slot so it can be returned to this setting
   for regular sewing.) If you prefer, keep
   an extra bobbin case on hand to use
   for bobbin work.
4. To place appliqué in embroidery
   hoop, lay outer hoop on flat surface,
   place appliqué, wrong side up, atop

outer hoop, and insert inner hoop.
Lower or cover feed dogs and put a
darning foot on your machine to
prepare for free-motion stitching.

5. As you begin stitching, hold threads
   firmly rather than making anchor
   stitches. Using the previous stitching
   as a guide, stitch around appliqué
   shapes as if you were sketching them
   (*Photo C*). Stitch double veins in large
   flower petals and short double center
   veins in leaves. Stitch a wavy line over
   stems and add wavy stems connecting
   smaller leaves to fabric stems. Leave a
   3"–4" tail of pearl cotton.

C

6. Using a chenille or tapestry needle, pull pearl cotton tail to wrong side (*Photo D*). Knot with back thread, trim thread tails to ½", and secure to back with fabric glue.

Sew **Smart**™

- Practice bobbin work on a sample to find proper tension.
- Bobbin thread will not come up and meet top thread at the normal halfway point in fabric.
- Thicker thread looks more interesting if it does not lie flat and smooth and has some indent where top thread catches bottom thread (*Photo E*). Tighten top tension if necessary, to achieve desired look.
- Speed of stitching and movement of the fabric will also affect the look of the bobbin thread. —Janet

DESIGNER

Janet Pittman translates her love of gardening to art quilts and quilt patterns. Her pattern company, Garden Trellis Designs, specializes in machine appliqué and fabric embellishment. Her book, *Appliqué The basics and beyond,* was published by Landauer Books. ✳

QUILT DESIGNED BY **John Flynn**.
MADE BY **Diane Ide**. MACHINE QUILTED BY **Dawn Cavanaugh**.

Double Wedding Ring

Make this traditional quilt in assorted batiks
for a contemporary twist. To cut your fabric pieces,
use our patterns for templates or purchase a set of rotary cutting
templates. See the *Sew Easy* lessons on pages 124 and 126 for
tips on piecing the quilt and attaching the binding.

PROJECT RATING: CHALLENGING

Size: 92⅝" × 105"

Blocks: 56 (18") rings

MATERIALS

½ yard each of 26 assorted bright
batiks for rings

6½ yards tan batik for background

⅞ yard blue batik for binding

Fons & Porter Double Wedding
Ring Template set or template
material

8¼ yards backing fabric

King-size quilt batting

Cutting

Patterns for templates are on page 127.
Measurements include ¼" seam
allowance.

From each bright batik, cut:

• 40 A.

• 10 B.

• 10 B reversed.

• 10 C.

From tan batik, cut:

• 127 D.

• 56 E.

From blue print batik, cut:

• 2"-wide bias strips. Join to make
about 450" of bias for binding.

Block Assembly

NOTE: Refer to *Sew Easy: Piecing Double Wedding Ring* on page 124 for detailed instructions, step-by-step photos, and sewing tips.

1. Referring to *Melon Unit Assembly* on page 124, join pieces to make 1 Melon Unit (*Melon Unit Diagrams*). Make 127 Melon Units.

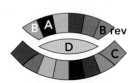

Melon Unit Diagrams

2. Referring to *Block Unit Diagrams*, below, and Block Unit Assembly instructions in *Sew Easy: Piecing Double Wedding Ring* on page 125, join 2 Melon Units to 1 E piece to complete 1 Block Unit. Make 56 Block Units.

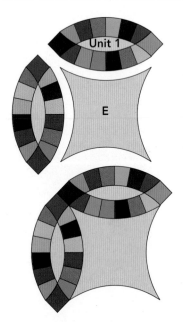

Block Unit Diagrams

Quilt Assembly

1. Lay out Melon Units and Block Units as shown in *Quilt Top Assembly Diagram*.

2. Referring to *Quilt Assembly* instructions on page 125, join units into rows. Join rows.

Finishing

1. Divide backing into 3 (2¾-yard) pieces. Join panels lengthwise; seams will run horizontally.

2. Layer backing, batting, and quilt top; baste. Quilt as desired. Quilt shown was quilted in the ditch in the rings and with feather designs in the background. (Feather motifs designed by Dawn Cavanaugh are given as dashed lines on template patterns on page 127.)

3. Referring to *Sew Easy: Binding Uneven Edges* on page 126, add binding to quilt.

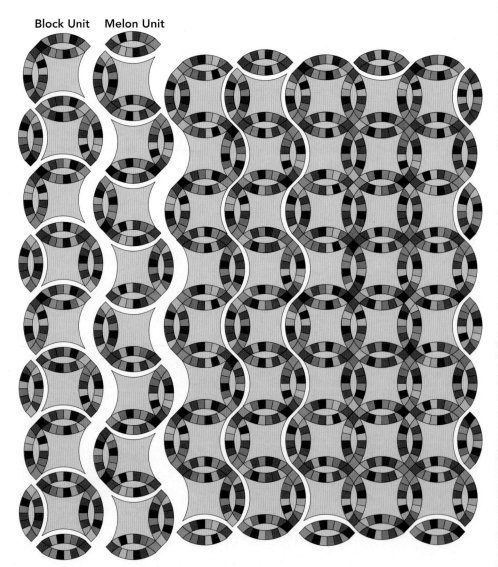

Quilt Top Assembly Diagram

We have included several variations to show possible color arrangements. ✳

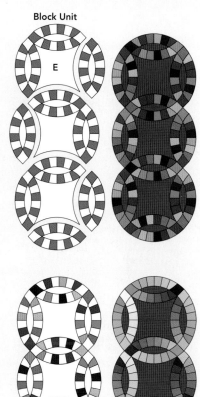

Block Unit

E

Make a table runner with just three rings

To make the 1930s version, pictured below, you need 1 yard of background fabric plus scraps of assorted prints and two solids. You also need batting, and fabric for backing and binding.

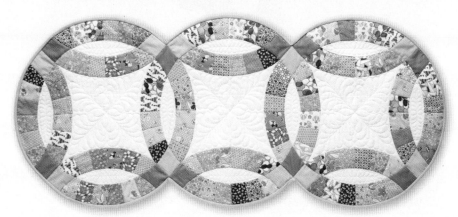

Cutting (for 3 rings)
From background fabric, cut:
  3 E.
  10 D.
From assorted prints, cut:
  80 A.
  20 B.
  20 B reversed.
From each of 2 solids, cut:
  10 C.

Sew *Easy*™

Piecing Double Wedding Ring

Piecing a Double Wedding Ring quilt is easier than it first appears, once you know a few tricks. You'll find the quilt goes together smoothly as you get more practice at managing the curved seams and matching the critical points.

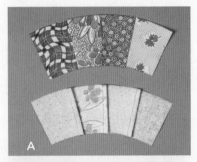

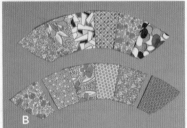

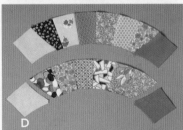

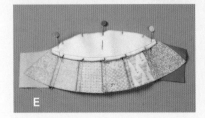

Melon Unit Assembly

1. Join 4 A wedges (*Photo A*).
2. Add B piece to 1 end of arc and B reverse piece to opposite end to complete 1 arc (*Photo B*). Make 2 arcs. With arc right side up, press seam allowances to the left.
3. Pin D melon to arc, matching ends and center, adding additional pins as desired (*Photo C*). With the melon on top, stitch melon to arc. Press seam allowances toward arc.
4. Add 1 C corner piece to each end of remaining arc (*Photo D*). (If you are using 2 colors for corner pieces, add a different colored C piece to each end.) Press seams toward corner pieces.
5. Working with the melon on top, pin intersections where C corner pieces meet adjacent arc (*Photo E*). Align edges of B and C pieces; stitch to first corner intersection, stopping with needle in fabric (*Photo F*). Lift presser foot and adjust fabric, aligning edge of melon to arc. Stitch to other corner intersection, stop with needle down, raise presser foot, align edges, and finish seam to complete Melon Unit.

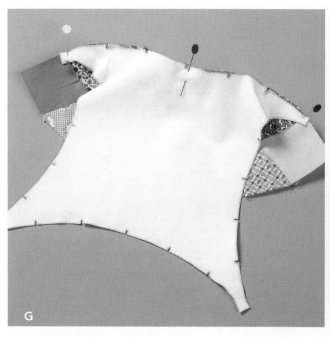

G

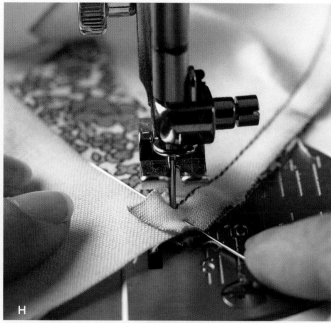

H

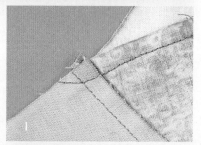

I

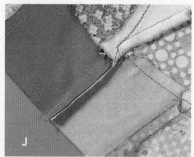

J

Block Unit Assembly

The basic piecing Unit for a Double Wedding Ring quilt is a center piece with Melon Units added to adjacent sides.

1. Working with the center piece on top, pin 1 Melon Unit to top edge of center piece. Pin at center and ¼" from ends *(Photo G)*.

2. Sew in at a 45-degree angle to the first pin, stop with needle down, raise presser foot, pivot, and sew along curved edge to the opposite end pin. Stop and pivot as before *(Photo H)* and sew off the end at a 45-degree angle. The angled beginning and ends of seams *(Photo I)* will allow you to chain piece as you assemble units. **Do not press seams until second Melon Unit has been added.**

3. With center piece on top, pin second Melon Unit to left edge of center piece, matching intersections of C corner pieces. Holding seam allowance of bottom C piece out of the way, stitch to intersection, backstitch, and remove

from machine. Align edge of center piece with melon. Stitch in from corner at 45-degree angle. With needle down, stop at intersection, lift presser foot, and adjust fabric. Stitch curved seam. At the end corner intersection, pivot and sew off the corner at an angle *(Photo J)*. Press seams toward arcs.

> ### Sew **Smart**™
>
> If you are using two colors for contrasting C corners, you will need to make an equal number of two slightly different block units (Block X and Block Y) with opposite color placement of the corner C pieces *(Photo K)*. —John

Quilt Assembly

1. Lay out Block Units in rows. (If you are using contrasting corners, alternate the two types of blocks in each row.)

2. Join Block Units into rows. Join rows. Add Melon Units to fill in outer edge of quilt.

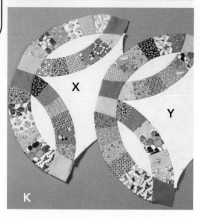

X Y

K

Binding Uneven Edges

Use this technique to bind a quilt that has inside corners or scalloped edges.

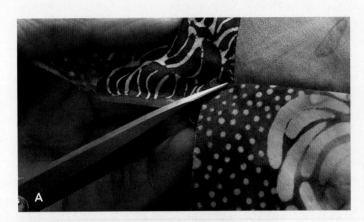

1. Trim batting and backing even with quilt top. At inside corners, clip almost to a quarter inch from edge (*Photo A*).

> ## Sew **Smart**™
>
> If your quilting does not go all the way to the edge of the quilt, use a walking foot to baste the layers together about ⅛" from the edge before trimming the quilt.
> —Marianne

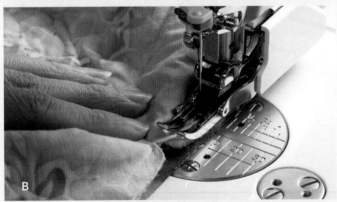

2. With binding on bottom and quilt back side up, use a walking foot to stitch binding to quilt ¼" from edge. At inside corners, pull on clipped area to straighten the quilt (*Photo B*). Be sure stitching clears the clipped area.
3. Fold binding to back of quilt. At the inside corners, fold the binding to create a miter (*Photo C*). Hand stitch binding to quilt back, stitching mitered fold at inside corners.

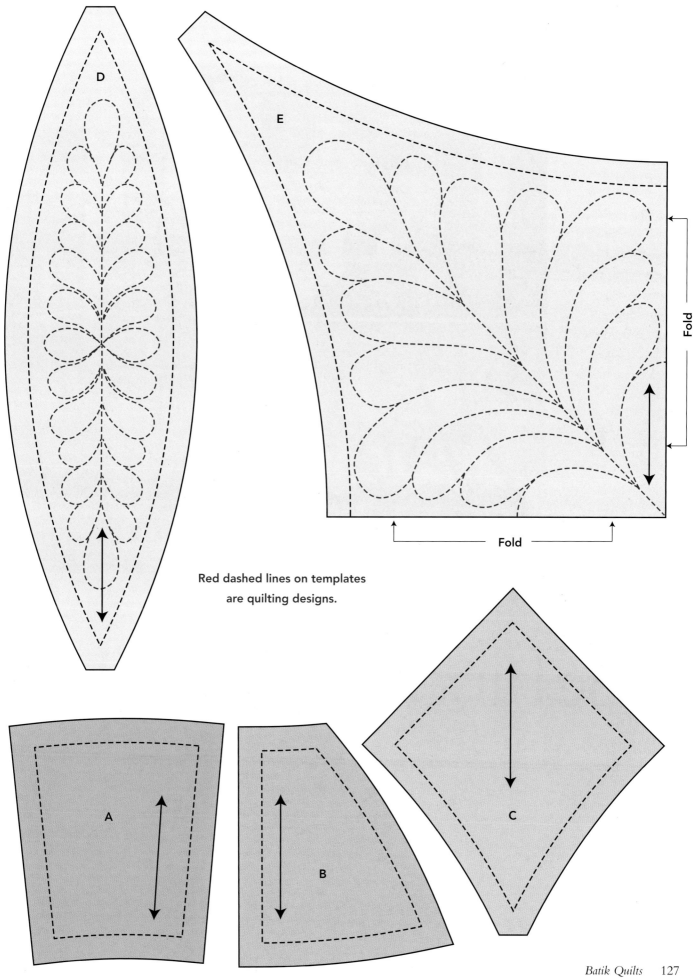

D

E

Fold

Fold

Red dashed lines on templates
are quilting designs.

C

A

B

Skilled Indonesian artisans, such as the man shown measuring dye, create the beautiful colors and motifs for the batiks American quilters adore. Fabrics go through many steps in the batiking process before they are rolled onto tubes and boxed for export to the United States.

BY **Bruce Magidson**.

Behind the Batiks

If you are passionate about textiles with exotic color and texture,
chances are you have a special love for batiks.

A

B

C

Fabric aficionados (also known as quilters) are universally captivated by the stunning, color-saturated batiks available online, at their local quilt shop, or from vendors at quilting events.

While there's always a place for a new "Bali" in a batik lover's stash, few know much about the fascinating, time-honored processes used to make batik fabrics. To help you understand how batiks are made, I'd like to take you on a visual trip to an Indonesian batik factory near the city of Solo, Indonesia.

Batik making is an ancient art for embellishing cloth through the use of wax (or other substance that creates a resist) and dyes. While batiks are produced in India, China, Thailand, and several African nations, the process is most renowned in Indonesia and Malaysia. In these areas, two basic processes are used to produce batik fabric: *batik tulis* (hand drawn batik) and *batik cap* (stamped batik). Most of the fabrics you will find in your local quilt shop are stamped ones, so I've focused on that method for this article.

Stamping involves the application of molten wax to cloth using a metal or wooden stamp called a *cap* (pronounced *chap*). The cap *(Photo A)* is a cookie cutter type device that has the batik motif it will produce worked on it in copper. In Indonesia, the cap is fabricated by local craftsmen who painstakingly follow the image given them by the customer.

Cloth Preparation

Before printing, impurities and starch are first removed from raw fabric. Often this is done before the cloth arrives at the batik factory.

Base Color

Once raw fabric is clean, base color may be applied before the waxing step. Base colors fill the surface area inside motif positions eventually shaped by the wax resist. The application of base color is often done with the fabric placed on the factory floor *(Photo B)*.

Wax Application

After base colors have been applied, the fabric is draped over a padded table so it will take the pressure of the stamp well. Blocks of wax *(Photo C)* are placed in a pot called a *wajan,* atop a small barbecue-like stove *(Photo D)* for melting. Once the wax is melted to the proper consistency, it can be applied

to the fabric. The batik artisan dips a stamp into the wajan to cover the stamp surface with molten wax. He then applies the stamp to the cloth *(Photo E)*. The artisan must carefully dovetail each wax impression with the ones he has already created to avoid gaps in the repeat *(Photo F)*.

Dyeing

After wax has been applied, the cloth is ready to be overdyed. Dyes are carefully color mixed and matched by factory workers and then applied in large cement dye baths *(Photo G)*. Areas that were covered by wax will resist the dyes and will become the desired motifs.

The dyeing process is repeated several times, depending on the number of colors and complexity of the design. Occasionally, a final application of black or other dark color is made to emphasize the design elements of the pattern.

Wax Removal

After the cloth has been rinsed and dried, the wax is removed entirely by dipping the fabric in hot water *(Photo H)*. Often, the wax itself is saved and reused. The cloth is then washed with a mild detergent, rinsed to remove excess dye *(Photo I)*, and hung in the sun to dry. Finally, the finished fabric is rolled on tubes for shipment.

The Future of Batik

While Indonesian batik making has been going on for centuries, it is undergoing a period of dynamic change because of demand.

Old batik techniques are being given new applications, and new base fabrics expand the potential uses of batik. Western companies now offer 108"-wide batik backing, batik flannel, silk batik, and many new thematic groups of stamped batik and hand-dyed batiks. It's an exciting time of renewal for this ancient fabric making process. Batik lovers will not be disappointed!

Author Profile

Bruce Magidson is co-founder of SewBatik, a direct marketer of batik and hand-dyed fabrics. Bruce oversees batik design, production, and import logistics. He has a BA from Rutgers University and a JD from Southwestern University School of Law. Bruce and his wife, Diane, reside in Hillsboro, North Dakota. ✳

General Instructions

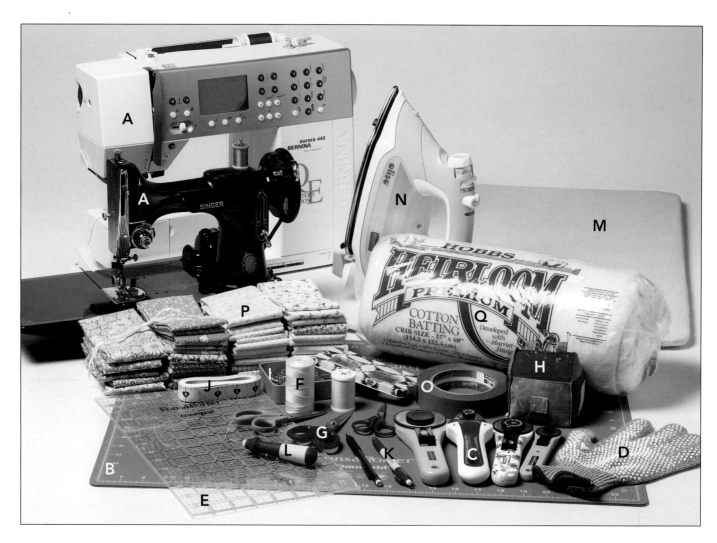

Basic Supplies

You'll need a **sewing machine (A)** in good working order to construct patchwork blocks, join blocks together, add borders, and machine quilt. We encourage you to purchase a machine from a local dealer, who can help you with service in the future, rather than from a discount store. Another option may be to borrow a machine from a friend or family member. If the machine has not been used in a while, have it serviced by a local dealer to make sure it is in good working order. If you need an extension cord, one with a surge protector is a good idea.

A **rotary cutting mat (B)** is essential for accurate and safe rotary cutting. Purchase one that is no smaller than 18" × 24".

Rotary cutting mats are made of "self-healing" material that can be used over and over.

A **rotary cutter (C)** is a cutting tool that looks like a pizza cutter, and has a very sharp blade. We recommend starting with a standard size 45mm rotary cutter. Always lock or close your cutter when it is not in use, and keep it out of the reach of children.

A **safety glove** (also known as a *Klutz Glove)* **(D)** is also recommended. Wear your safety glove on the hand that is holding the ruler in place. Because it is made of cut-resistant material, the safety glove protects your non-cutting hand from accidents that can occur if your cutting hand slips while cutting.

An acrylic **ruler (E)** is used in combination with your cutting mat and rotary cutter. We recommend the Fons & Porter

8" × 14" ruler, but a 6" × 12" ruler is another good option. You'll need a ruler with inch, quarter-inch, and eighth-inch markings that show clearly for ease of measuring. Choose a ruler with 45-degree-angle, 30-degree-angle, and 60-degree-angle lines marked on it as well.

Since you will be using 100% cotton fabric for your quilts, use **cotton or cotton-covered polyester thread (F)** for piecing and quilting. Avoid 100% polyester thread, as it tends to snarl.

Keep a pair of small **scissors (G)** near your sewing machine for cutting threads.

Thin, good quality **straight pins (H)** are preferred by quilters. The pins included with pin cushions are normally too thick to use for piecing, so discard them. Purchase a box of nickel-plated brass **safety pins** size #1 **(I)** to use for pin-basting the layers of your quilt together for machine quilting.

Invest in a 120"-long dressmaker's **measuring tape (J)**. This will come in handy when making borders for your quilt.

A 0.7–0.9mm mechanical **pencil (K)** works well for marking on your fabric.

Invest in a quality sharp **seam ripper (L)**. Every quilter gets well-acquainted with her seam ripper!

Set up an **ironing board (M)** and **iron (N)** in your sewing area. Pressing yardage before cutting, and pressing patchwork seams as you go are both essential for quality quiltmaking. Select an iron that has steam capability.

Masking **tape (O)** or painter's tape works well to mark your sewing machine so you can sew an accurate ¼" seam. You will also use tape to hold your backing fabric taut as you prepare your quilt sandwich for machine quilting.

The most exciting item that you will need for quilting is **fabric (P)**. Quilters generally prefer 100% cotton fabrics for their quilts. This fabric is woven from cotton threads, and has a lengthwise and a crosswise grain. The term "bias" is used to describe the diagonal grain of the fabric. If you make a 45-degree angle cut through a square of cotton fabric, the cut edges will be bias edges, which are quite stretchy. As you learn more quiltmaking techniques, you'll learn how bias can work to your advantage or disadvantage.

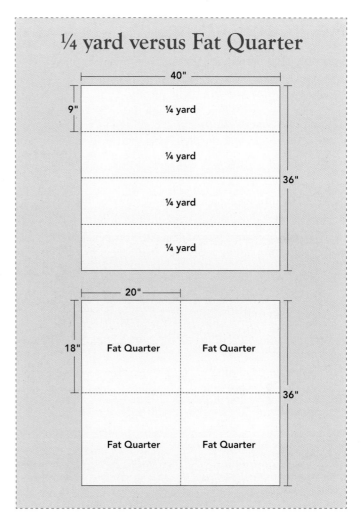

¼ yard versus Fat Quarter

Fabric is sold by the yard at quilt shops and fabric stores. Quilting fabric is generally about 40"–44" wide, so a yard is about 40" wide by 36" long. As you collect fabrics to build your own personal stash, you will buy yards, half yards (about 18" × 40"), quarter yards (about 9" × 40"), as well as other lengths.

Many quilt shops sell "fat quarters," a special cut favored by quilters. A fat quarter is created by cutting a half yard down the fold line into two 18" × 20" pieces (fat quarters) that are sold separately. Quilters like the nearly square shape of the fat quarter because it is more useful than the narrow regular quarter yard cut.

Batting (Q) is the filler between quilt top and backing that makes your quilt a quilt. It can be cotton, polyester, cotton-polyester blend, wool, silk, or other natural materials, such as bamboo or corn. Make sure the batting you buy is at least six inches wider and six inches longer than your quilt top.

Accurate Cutting

Measuring and cutting accuracy are important for successful quilting. Measure at least twice, and cut once!

Cut strips across the fabric width unless directed otherwise.

Cutting for patchwork usually begins with cutting strips, which are then cut into smaller pieces. First, cut straight strips from a fat quarter:

1. Fold fat quarter in half with selvage edge at the top (*Photo A*).

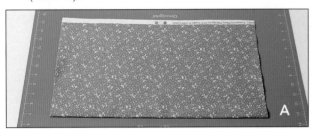

2. Straighten edge of fabric by placing ruler atop fabric, aligning one of the lines on ruler with selvage edge of fabric (*Photo B*). Cut along right edge of ruler.

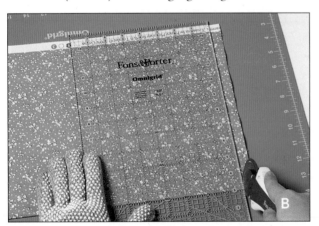

3. Rotate fabric, and use ruler to measure from cut edge to desired strip width (*Photo C*). Measurements in instructions include ¼" seam allowances.

4. After cutting the required number of strips, cut strips into squares and label them.

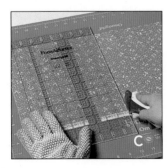

Setting up Your Sewing Machine

Sew Accurate ¼" Seams

Standard seam width for patchwork and quiltmaking is ¼". Some machines come with a patchwork presser foot, also known as a quarter-inch foot. If your machine doesn't have a quarter-inch foot, you may be able to purchase one from a dealer. Or, you can create a quarter-inch seam guide on your machine using masking tape or painter's tape.

Place an acrylic ruler on your sewing machine bed under the presser foot. Slowly turn handwheel until the tip of the needle barely rests atop the ruler's quarter-inch mark (*Photo A*). Make sure the lines on the ruler are parallel to the lines on the machine throat plate. Place tape on the machine bed along edge of ruler (*Photo B*).

Take a Simple Seam Test

Seam accuracy is critical to machine piecing, so take this simple test once you have your quarter-inch presser foot on your machine or have created a tape guide.

Place 2 (2½") squares right sides together, and sew with a scant ¼" seam. Open squares and finger press seam. To finger press, with right sides facing you, press the seam to one side with your fingernail. Measure across pieces, raw edge to raw edge (*Photo C*). If they measure 4½", you have passed the test! Repeat the test as needed to make sure you can confidently sew a perfect ¼" seam.

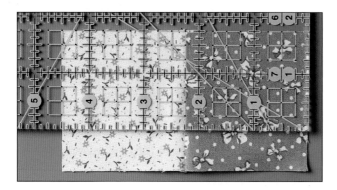

Sewing Comfortably

Other elements that promote pleasant sewing are good lighting, a comfortable chair, background music—and chocolate! Good lighting promotes accurate sewing. The better you can see what you are working on, the better your results. A comfortable chair enables you to sew for longer periods of time. An office chair with a good back rest and adjustable height works well. Music helps keep you relaxed. Chocolate is, for many quilters, simply a necessity.

Tips for Patchwork and Pressing

As you sew more patchwork, you'll develop your own shortcuts and favorite methods. Here are a few favored by many quilters:

● As you join patchwork units to form rows, and join rows to form blocks, press seams in opposite directions from row to row whenever possible (*Photo A*). By pressing seams one direction in the first row and the opposite direction in the next row, you will often create seam allowances that abut when rows are joined (*Photo B*). Abutting or nesting seams are ideal for forming perfectly matched corners on the right side of your quilt blocks and quilt top. Such pressing is not always possible, so don't worry if you end up with seam allowances facing the same direction as you join units.

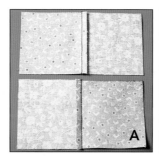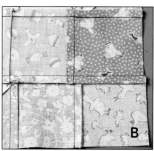

● Sew on and off a small, folded fabric square to prevent bobbin thread from bunching at throat plate (*Photo C*). You'll also save thread, which means fewer stops to wind bobbins, and fewer hanging threads to be snipped. Repeated use of the small piece of fabric gives it lots of thread "legs," so some quilters call it a spider.

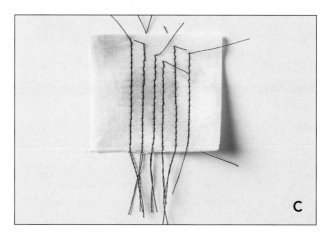

- Chain piece patchwork to reduce the amount of thread you use, and minimize the number and length of threads you need to trim from patchwork. Without cutting threads at the end of a seam, take 3–4 stitches without any fabric under the needle, creating a short thread chain approximately ⅛" long (*Photo D*). Repeat until you have a long line of pieces. Remove chain from machine, clip threads between units, and press seams.

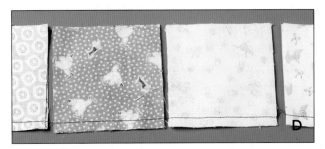

- Trim off tiny triangle tips (sometimes called dog ears) created when making triangle-square units (*Photo E*). Trimming triangles reduces bulk and makes patchwork units and blocks lie flatter. Though no one will see the back of your quilt top once it's quilted, a neat back free of dangling threads and patchwork points is the mark of a good quilter. Also, a smooth, flat quilt top is easier to quilt, whether by hand or machine.

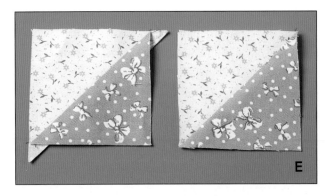

- Careful pressing will make your patchwork neat and crisp, and will help make your finished quilt top lie flat. Ironing and pressing are two different skills. Iron fabric to remove wrinkles using a back and forth, smoothing motion. Press patchwork and quilt blocks by raising and gently lowering the iron atop your work. After sewing a patchwork unit, first press the seam with the unit closed, pressing to set, or embed, the stitching. Setting the seam this way will help produce straight, crisp seams. Open the unit and press on the right side with the seam toward the darkest fabric, being careful to not form a pleat in your seam, and carefully pressing the patchwork flat.

- Many quilters use finger pressing to open and flatten seams of small units before pressing with an iron. To finger press, open patchwork unit with right side of fabric facing you. Run your fingernail firmly along seam, making sure unit is fully open with no pleat.

- Careful use of steam in your iron will make seams and blocks crisp and flat (*Photo F*). Aggressive ironing can stretch blocks out of shape, and is a common pitfall for new quilters.

Adding Borders

Follow these simple instructions to make borders that fit perfectly on your quilt.

1. Find the length of your quilt by measuring through the quilt center, not along the edges, since the edges may have stretched. Take 3 measurements and average them to determine the length to cut your side borders (*Diagram A*). Cut 2 side borders this length.

2. Fold border strips in half to find center. Pinch to create crease mark or place a pin at center. Fold quilt top in half crosswise to find center of side. Attach side borders to quilt center by pinning them at the ends and the center, and easing in any fullness. If quilt edge is a bit longer than border, pin and sew with border on top; if border is

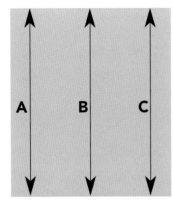

Diagram A

A _____

B _____

C _____

TOTAL _____

÷3

_____

AVERAGE
LENGTH _____

HELPFUL TIP
Use the following decimal conversions to calculate
your quilt's measurements:

⅛" = .125	⅝" = .625
¼" = .25	¾" = .75
⅜" = .375	⅞" = .875
½" = .5	

---

slightly longer than quilt top, pin and sew with border on the bottom. Machine feed dogs will ease in the fullness of the longer piece. Press seams toward borders.

3. Find the width of your quilt by measuring across the quilt and side borders (*Diagram B*). Take 3 measurements and average them to determine the length to cut your top and bottom borders. Cut 2 borders this length.

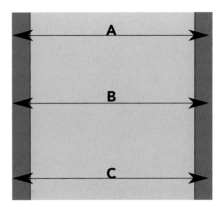

Diagram B

4. Mark centers of borders and top and bottom edges of quilt top. Attach top and bottom borders to quilt, pinnning at ends and center, and easing in any fullness (*Diagram C*). Press seams toward borders.

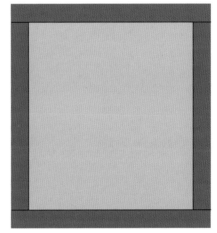

Diagram C

5. Gently steam press entire quilt top on one side and then the other. When pressing on wrong side, trim off any loose threads.

Joining Border Strips

Not all quilts have borders, but they are a nice complement to a quilt top. If your border is longer than 40", you will need to join 2 or more strips to make a border the required length. You can join border strips with either a straight seam parallel to the ends of the strips (*Photo A* on page 138), or with a diagonal seam. For the diagonal seam method, place one border strip perpendicular to another strip, rights sides facing (*Photo B*). Stitch diagonally across strips as shown. Trim seam allowance to ¼". Press seam open (*Photo C*).

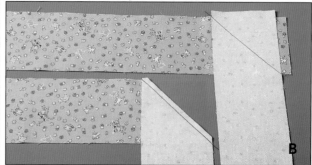

Quilting Your Quilt

Quilters today joke that there are three ways to quilt a quilt—by hand, by machine, or by check. Some enjoy making quilt tops so much, they prefer to hire a professional machine quilter to finish their work. The Split Nine Patch baby quilt shown at left has simple machine quilting that you can do yourself.

Decide what color thread will look best on your quilt top before choosing your backing fabric. A thread color that will blend in with the quilt top is a good choice for beginners. Choose backing fabric that will blend with your thread as well. A print fabric is a good choice for hiding less-than-perfect machine quilting. The backing fabric must be at least 3"–4" larger than your quilt top on all 4 sides. For example: if your quilt top measures 44" × 44", your backing needs to be at least 50" × 50". If your quilt top is 80" × 96", then your backing fabric needs to be at least 86" × 102".

For quilt tops 36" wide or less, use a single width of fabric for the backing. Buy enough length to allow adequate margin at quilt edges, as noted above. When your quilt is wider than 36", one option is to use 60"-, 90"-, or 108"-wide fabric for the quilt backing. Because fabric selection is limited for wide fabrics, quilters generally piece the quilt backing from 44/45"-wide fabric. Plan on 40"–42" of usable fabric width when estimating how much fabric to purchase. Plan your piecing strategy to avoid having a seam along the vertical or horizontal center of the quilt.

For a quilt 37"–60" wide, a backing with horizontal seams is usually the most economical use of fabric. For example, for a quilt 50" × 70", vertical seams would require 152", or 4¼ yards, of 44/45"-wide fabric (76" + 76" = 152"). Horizontal seams would require 112", or 3¼ yards (56" + 56" = 112").

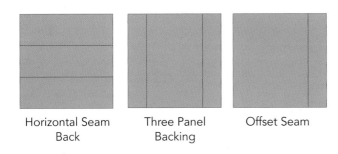

Horizontal Seam Back Three Panel Backing Offset Seam

For a quilt 61"–80" wide, most quilters piece a three-panel backing, with vertical seams, from two lengths of fabric. Cut one of the pieces in half lengthwise, and sew the halves to opposite sides of the wider panel. Press the seams away from the center panel.

For a quilt 81"–120" wide, you will need three lengths of fabric, plus extra margin. For example, for a quilt 108" × 108", purchase at least 342", or 9½ yards, of 44/45"-wide fabric (114" + 114" + 114" = 342").

For a three-panel backing, pin the selvage edge of the center panel to the selvage edge of the side panel, with edges aligned and right sides facing. Machine stitch with a ½" seam. Trim seam allowances to ¼", trimming off the selvages from both panels at once. Press the seam away from the center of the quilt. Repeat on other side of center panel.

For a two-panel backing, join panels in the same manner as above, and press the seam to one side.

Create a "quilt sandwich" by layering your backing, batting, and quilt top. Find the crosswise center of the backing fabric by folding it in half. Mark with a pin on each side. Lay backing down on a table or floor, wrong side up. Tape corners and edges of backing to the surface with masking or painter's tape so that backing is taut (*Photo A*).

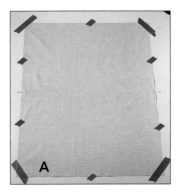

Fold batting in half crosswise and position it atop backing fabric, centering folded edge at center of backing (*Photo B*). Unfold batting and smooth it out atop backing (*Photo C*).

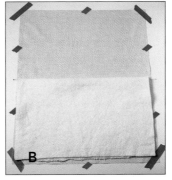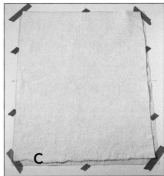

In the same manner, fold the quilt top in half crosswise and center it atop backing and batting (*Photo D*). Unfold top and smooth it out atop batting (*Photo E*).

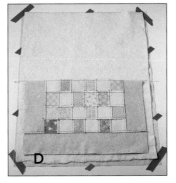

Use safety pins to pin baste the layers (*Photo F*). Pins should be about a fist width apart. A special tool, called a Kwik Klip, or a grapefruit spoon makes closing the pins easier. As you slide a pin through all three layers, slide the point of the pin into one of the tool's grooves. Push on the tool to help close the pin.

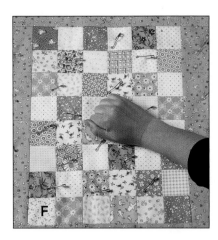

For straight line quilting, install an even feed or walking foot on your machine. This presser foot helps all three layers of your quilt move through the machine evenly without bunching.

Walking Foot

Stitching "in the ditch"

An easy way to quilt your first quilt is to stitch "in the ditch" along seam lines. No marking is needed for this type of quilting.

Binding Your Quilt

Preparing Binding

Strips for quilt binding may be cut either on the straight of grain or on the bias.

1. Measure the perimeter of your quilt and add approximately 24" to allow for mitered corners and finished ends.
2. Cut the number of strips necessary to achieve desired length. We like to cut binding strips 2¼" wide.
3. Join your strips with diagonal seams into 1 continuous piece (*Photo A*). Press the seams open. (See page 142 for instructions for the diagonal seams method of joining strips.)

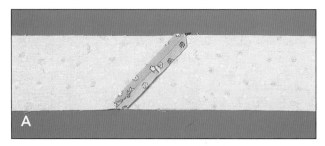

4. Press your binding in half lengthwise, with wrong sides facing, to make French-fold binding (*Photo B*).

Attaching Binding

Attach the binding to your quilt using an even-feed or walking foot. This prevents puckering when sewing through the three layers.

1. Choose beginning point along one side of quilt. Do not start at a corner. Match the two raw edges of the binding strip to the raw edge of the quilt top. The folded edge

will be free and to left of seam line (*Photo C*). Leave 12" or longer tail of binding strip dangling free from beginning point. Stitch, using ¼" seam, through all layers.

2. For mitered corners, stop stitching ¼" from corner; backstitch, and remove quilt from sewing machine (*Photo D*). Place a pin ¼" from corner to mark where you will stop stitching.

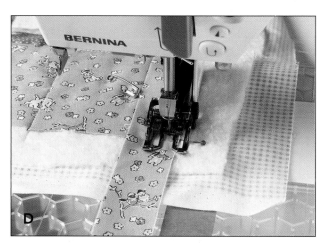

Rotate quilt quarter turn and fold binding straight up, away from corner, forming 45-degree-angle fold (*Photo E*).

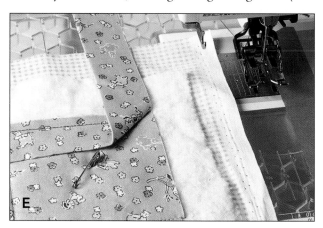

Bring binding straight down in line with next edge to be sewn, leaving top fold even with raw edge of previously sewn side (*Photo F*). Begin stitching at top edge, sewing through all layers (*Photo G*).

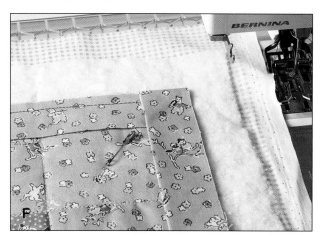

3. To finish binding, stop stitching about 8" away from starting point, leaving about a 12" tail at end (*Photo H*). Bring beginning and end of binding to center of 8" opening and fold each back, leaving about ¼" space

between the two folds of binding (*Photo I*). (Allowing this ¼" extra space is critical, as binding tends to stretch when it is stitched to the quilt. If the folded ends meet at this point, your binding will be too long for the space after the ends are joined.) Crease folds of binding with your fingernail.

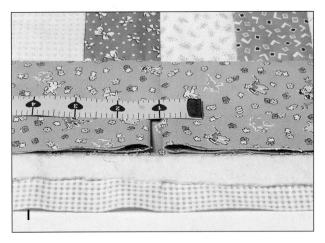

4. Open out each edge of binding and draw line across wrong side of binding on creased fold line, as shown in *Photo J*. Draw line along lengthwise fold of binding at same spot to create an X (*Photo K*).

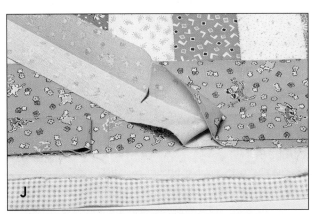

5. With edge of ruler at marked X, line up 45-degree-angle marking on ruler with one long side of binding (*Photo L*). Draw diagonal line across binding as shown in *Photo M*.

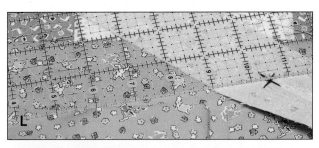

Repeat for other end of binding. Lines must angle in same direction (*Photo N*).

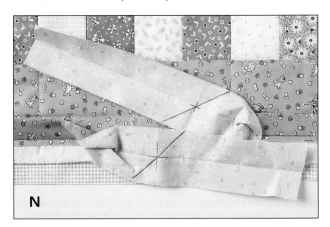

6. Pin binding ends together with right sides facing, pin-matching diagonal lines as shown in *Photo O*. Binding ends will be at right angles to each other. Machine-stitch along diagonal line, removing pins as you stitch (*Photo P*).

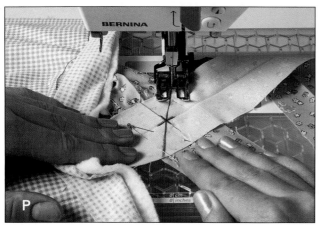

7. Lay binding against quilt to double-check that it is correct length (*Photo Q*). Trim ends of binding ¼" from diagonal seam (*Photo R*).

8. Finger press diagonal seam open (*Photo S*). Fold binding in half and finish stitching binding to quilt (*Photo T*).

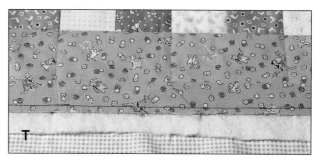

Hand Stitching Binding to Quilt Back

1. Trim any excess batting and quilt back with scissors or a rotary cutter (*Photo A*). Leave enough batting (about ⅛" beyond quilt top) to fill binding uniformly when it is turned to quilt back.

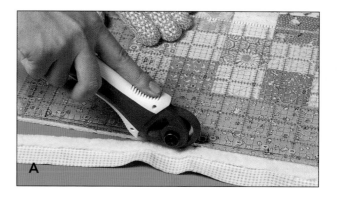

2. Bring folded edge of binding to quilt back so that it covers machine stitching. Blindstitch folded edge to quilt backing, using a few pins just ahead of stitching to hold binding in place (*Photo B*).

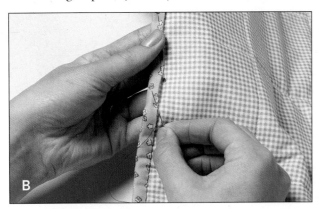

3. Continue stitching to corner. Fold unstitched binding from next side under, forming a 45-degree angle and a mitered corner. Stitch mitered folds on both front and back (*Photo C*).

Finishing Touches

- **Label your quilt so the recipient and future generations know who made it.** To make a label, use a fabric marking pen to write the details on a small piece of solid color fabric (*Photo A*). To make writing easier, put pieces of masking tape on the wrong side. Remove tape after writing. Use your iron to turn under ¼" on each edge, then stitch the label to the back of your quilt using a blindstitch, taking care not to sew through to quilt top.

- **Take a photo of your quilt.** Keep your photos in an album or journal along with notes, fabric swatches, and other information about the quilts.

- **If your quilt is a gift, include care instructions.** Some quilt shops carry pre-printed care labels you can sew onto the quilt (*Photo B*). Or, make a care label using the method described above.